The NCTE High School Literature Series

The NCTE High School Literature Series offers classroom teachers in-depth studies of individual writers. Grounded in theory, each volume focuses on a single author or work and features excerpts from the writer's works, biographical information, and samples of professional literary criticism. Rich in opportunities for classroom discussion and writing assignments that teachers can adapt to their own literature curriculum, each book also offers many examples of student writing.

Volumes in the Series

The Great Gatsby *in the Classroom: Searching for the American Dream* (2006), David Dowling

Judith Ortiz Cofer in the Classroom: A Woman in Front of the Sun (2006), Carol Jago

Langston Hughes in the Classroom: "Do Nothin' till You Hear from Me" (2006), Carmaletta M. Williams

Amy Tan in the Classroom: "The art of invisible strength" (2005), Renée H. Shea and Deborah L. Wilchek

Raymond Carver in the Classroom: "A Small, Good Thing" (2005), Susanne Rubenstein

Sandra Cisneros in the Classroom: "Do not forget to reach" (2002), Carol Jago

Alice Walker in the Classroom: "Living by the Word" (2000), Carol Jago

Nikki Giovanni in the Classroom: "The same ol danger but a brand new pleasure" (1999), Carol Jago

Tim O'Brien in the Classroom

"This too is true: Stories can save us"

The NCTE High School Literature Series

Barry Gilmore

Lausanne Collegiate School

Memphis, Tennessee

Alexander Kaplan

Newton South High School

Newton, Massachusetts

National Council of Teachers of English
1111 W. Kenyon Road, Urbana, Illinois 61801-1096

Staff Editor: Bonny Graham
Interior Design: Jenny Jensen Greenleaf
Cover Design: Jenny Jensen Greenleaf and Tom Jaczak
Cover photo © Marion Ettlinger

NCTE Stock Number: 54663
ISSN 1525-5786

It is the policy of NCTE in its journals and other publications to provide a forum for the open discussion of ideas concerning the content and the teaching of English and the language arts. Publicity accorded to any particular point of view does not imply endorsement by the Executive Committee, the Board of Directors, or the membership at large, except in announcements of policy, where such endorsement is clearly specified.

Every effort has been made to provide current URLs and email addresses, but because of the rapidly changing nature of the Web, some sites and addresses may no longer be accessible.

Library of Congress Cataloging-in-Publication Data

Gilmore, Barry.
    Tim O'Brien in the classroom : this too is true : stories can save us / Barry Gilmore ; Alexander Kaplan.
        p. cm. — (NCTE high school literature series)
    Includes bibliographical references.
    ISBN 978-0-8141-5466-3 (pbk.)
    1. O'Brien, Tim, 1946—Study and teaching (Secondary) 2. Vietnam War, 1961–1975—Literature and the war—Study and teaching. 3. War stories, American—Study and teaching. I. Kaplan, Alexander, 1970– II. National Council of Teachers of English. III. Title.
PS3565.B75Z63 2007
813' .54—dc22

                                                            2007033767

Contents

5. Taking a Critical Stance

This chapter includes reviews and critical analyses of Tim O'Brien's work. Students develop their own ideas about O'Brien's work and how to respond to it by reading what others have written and said about the novels and stories. Suggestions for essay topics are included.

6. The Author's Voice: Interviews and Recollections

Tim O'Brien answers questions about his life and work.

7. Extensions and Connections

The ideas inherent in war stories offer rich connections to other material in the literary canon. This chapter offers avenues for exploring more of O'Brien's work and for pairing that work with traditionally taught novels, poems, and plays.

Introduction

In a lecture at Southwest Texas State University in the spring of 2000, Tim O'Brien said, "Stories are not explanations of the world we live in[;] . . . science does that, and math does that. Our obligation as fiction writers is to enhance the mysteries" (Hepola). Time and again, when we expose our students to O'Brien's work, it is those mysteries that elicit the most response. Girls who claim not to like stories about war or violence as well as boys who can't get enough of blood and gore (or the reverse) are drawn to the gray areas of O'Brien's stories, the parts that have more to do with human experience than with a specific time period or political stance.

Having knowledge of O'Brien's work, especially *The Things They Carried* and individual stories from it, is a great asset for English and creative writing teachers. His stories fit several potential teaching units—fiction of Vietnam, first-person narratives, important stories or novels from the last twenty-five years, metafiction, war stories, story cycles, or unconventional narrative structures. Additionally, they can serve to initiate discussions about the reliability of memory, the purpose of storytelling, or where fiction comes from.

In the spirit of the other books in the NCTE High School Literature Series, we've focused on opportunities for classroom discussion and writing assignments. A twelfth-grade English teacher adding a companion novel for *Heart of Darkness* to the curriculum doesn't have the same needs as a creative writing teacher looking for a few linked short stories; with the range of curricula that might include

O'Brien's works in mind, we have put together lessons, open-ended prompts, and student writing samples as starting points for teachers. We hope this less prescriptive and more suggestive approach gives you the flexibility to apply areas and methods that have been successful for us in sparking student interest to your own classroom.

A quick note about our use of the first person: although the authors taught right across the hall from each other, we did not teach the same course as a team. For several years, Barry has taught twelfth-grade English and Advanced Placement English Literature, and for four of those years Alex taught eleventh-grade English and Advanced Placement English Language with a focus on American literature, in addition to electives in creative writing and short fiction. Even though each of us has different approaches to O'Brien's work, his writing has fit well into lesson plans in all of our courses, and we've frequently collaborated and shared many of the methods you'll find in this volume. Even though some approaches have been used mainly by only one of us, for the sake of uniformity in the book, the pronoun *we* stands for both authors, Alex and Barry.

Finally, for the purposes of this book, we've narrowed our discussion largely to *The Things They Carried*, which is not a linear story. Its chronology is jumbled, its styles change, and its narratives vary in length and depth from story to story. Several issues worthy of our attention—and of the attention of English and creative writing teachers—come up throughout O'Brien's book, and we could have started with any one of them; here, rather than working through a single novel from beginning to end, we've chosen to use stories and novels by O'Brien as examples of salient literary points teachers might wish to discuss. Because each chapter mentions several of the stories, we've provided a chapter-by-chapter list of those stories mentioned in an appendix at the end of the book. We hope this will provide an easy guide when you want to teach an individual story. Each of those mentions, however, is just a jumping-off point for your class; most of the things we cover could be brought up in a discussion of every one of the stories in the book.

O'Brien's novels have provided rich ground for our English and creative writing classes. His stories resonate with students on both intellectual and emotional levels and prompt classes to make important connections between the historical and the personal, between style and idea, between memory and storytelling. If the reassuring statement that "stories can save us" from the last chapter of *The Things They Carried* is true, it's been our experience that O'Brien's own stories—and the stories students write on their own as a result of reading his work—are well-suited for the job.

1 Where Life and Art Intersect

> *By telling stories, you objectify your own experience. You sepa-*
> *rate it from yourself. You pin down certain truths. You make*
> *up others.* (The Things They Carried 158)

Even among a select group of writers whose lives seem closely tied to their writings about war—Ernest Hemingway, Wilfred Owen, Joseph Heller—Tim O'Brien stands out. When students read an O'Brien novel, usually *The Things They Carried*, the first question they tend to ask is both obvious and important: "How much of this is true?" Though they don't always know it at the time, that question is fundamental to understanding the author's works. How does one separate fact and fiction when an author names his narrator after himself, dedicates a work to his fictional characters, or tells us at one point that a story is absolutely true and at another that he made it up? How much is true? Tim O'Brien himself has offered some complicated answers, and the entire second chapter of this book is dedicated to exploring the careful line O'Brien walks between truth and fiction.

Yet the easy answer to the question is, "Some of it is true." Definite facts about O'Brien's life are reflected in the backgrounds of his characters and stories. The most important of these facts is that O'Brien served as a foot soldier in Vietnam; all of his writing, to some degree, is influenced by that experience. But O'Brien's life before the war informs many of his stories as well. Born in 1946 in Worthington, Minnesota, a town that labeled itself "Turkey Capital of the World," O'Brien grew up surrounded by the values and lessons of Middle America. Here is how he describes his birthplace in his memoir, *If I Die in a Combat Zone*:

> Among these people I learned about the Second World War, hearing it from men in front of the courthouse, from those who had fought it. The talk was tough. Nothing to do with causes or reason; the war was right, they muttered, and it had to be fought. The talk was about bellies filled with German lead, about the long hike from Normandy to Berlin, about close calls and about the origin of scars just visible on hairy arms. Growing up, I learned about another war, a peninsular war in Korea, a gray war fought by the town's Lutherans and Baptists. I learned about that war when the town hero came home, riding in a convertible, sitting straight-backed and quiet, an ex-POW. (13)

In 1968, O'Brien graduated from Macalester College with a degree in political science. The war in Vietnam was already under way; during his college years, O'Brien had attended protests and peace vigils and had planned to join the State Department. In an interview with *Ploughshares* (Lee), he says, "I thought we needed people who were progressive and had the patience to try diplomacy instead of dropping bombs on people."

Then O'Brien was drafted and assigned to infantry service. Certainly, he questioned the value of the war and his role in it. His books contain multiple accounts of plans to dodge the draft by fleeing to Canada. In his story "On the Rainy River," the fictional storyteller Tim O'Brien describes the pressure of "all those eyes on me—the town, the whole universe" (*The Things They Carried* 59). It's hard not to imagine that the paradox this narrator uses to sum up the experience squares with O'Brien's own feelings about his service: "I survived," the storyteller says, "but it's not a happy ending. I was a coward. I went to the war" (61).

In 1970, O'Brien returned from the war with a Purple Heart and, while completing graduate work at Harvard, began to write. His first book, *If I Die in a Combat Zone, Box Me Up and Ship Me Home*, was published in 1973, followed by novels published every few years throughout the next three decades. One of these, *Going After Cacciato,* was awarded the National Book Award in 1979, but it was the 1990 publication of *The Things They Carried* (a finalist for the Pulitzer Prize) that prompted *New York Times* reviewer Robert R. Harris to state:

> [He] captures the war's pulsating rhythms and nerve-racking dangers. But he goes much further. By moving beyond the horror of the fighting to examine with sensitivity and insight the nature of courage and fear, by questioning the role that imagination plays in helping to form our memories and our own versions of truth, he places "The Things They Carried" high up on the list of best fiction about any war.

Because it is as much a book about storytelling and the nature of fiction and truth as it is a war novel, *The Things They Carried* has made its way into more and more secondary and college classrooms and anthologies. The first story in the book, "The Things They Carried," straightforwardly catalogs the items carried by foot soldiers in the war. This excerpt from the second paragraph of the story serves as a good example of both the description and the narrative style:

> The things they carried were largely determined by necessity. Among the necessities or near-necessities were P-38 can open-

ers, pocket knives, heat tabs, wristwatches, dog tags, mosquito repellent, chewing gum, candy, cigarettes, salt tablets, packets of Kool-Aid, lighters, matches, sewing kits, Military Payment Certificates, C rations, and two or three canteens of water. Together, these items weighed between 15 and 20 pounds, depending upon a man's habits or rate of metabolism. Henry Dobbins, who was a big man, carried extra rations; he was especially fond of canned peaches in heavy syrup over pound cake. Dave Jensen, who practiced field hygiene, carried a toothbrush, dental floss, and several hotel-sized bars of soap he'd stolen on R&R in Sydney, Australia. Ted Lavender, who was scared, carried tranquilizers until he was shot in the head outside the village of Than Khe in mid-April. By necessity, and because it was SOP, they all carried steel helmets that weighed 5 pounds including the liner and camouflage cover. They carried the standard fatigue jackets and trousers. Very few carried underwear. On their feet they carried jungle boots—2.1 pounds—and Dave Jensen carried three pairs of socks and a can of Dr. Scholl's foot powder as a precaution against trench foot. (2–3)

Reading *The Things They Carried*

Before they read "The Things They Carried," have your students make a list of every object, however insignificant, they are carrying in their pockets, purses, or backpacks. When they're done, ask for two or three volunteers to read their lists aloud. Then ask them to think about—or fast-write about—what their lists might reveal or suggest to an outside observer about their character, their values, or their background.

Then read the beginning of the story out loud; we prefer to have various students read a paragraph each until the class finishes the first four or five sections of the story, about one quarter of the whole story (students can finish the story by reading silently in class or for homework). We also recommend, before beginning to read, discussing with students their expectations for the language and content of a story about Vietnam and preparing them to be mature readers (for a more complete discussion of dealing with O'Brien's language and possible challenges to the book, see Chapter 4).

Discussion

Students may wish to share their reactions to the start of the story as soon as the class finishes reading—certainly, the descriptions may call to mind other works or movies, stories members of the class have heard from parents or relatives who served in a war, or questions about the nature of the Vietnam War itself. It's worthwhile to let an organic discussion about the story develop, but also try to guide students gently so that they address the following two questions:

- *How much of the story do you think is true?* Tim O'Brien does not actually name himself as a character until the second story in this book; "The Things They Carried" is framed as a third-person narrative, yet the meticulous detail of the story suggests a level of personal experience that would be hard to duplicate. To prepare your students to read the rest of the novel, ask them which parts they think are based on the author's memory of actual lists, characters, and experiences. Then have them revisit their own lists of personal items they are carrying. Are there items that are misleading on these lists, or items that students often carry (but aren't at the moment) that might reveal more about their personalities? If they were trying to cast themselves as characters in a story, would they alter the lists in any way? If so, would a list with five items a student is actually carrying and one item he or she is not be more or less "true" than the original list?

■ *What tools does O'Brien use to make these lists more revealing about the characters and the war itself?* Some students may finish the first section of "The Things They Carried" and complain that "it's just a bunch of lists." In answer to this complaint, and as preparation for students' own writing, have students read closely in the first sections of the story to identify the following narrative devices:

◆ *Earned abstractions.* One of the greatest challenges for high school writers is learning the value of concrete imagery and that the rare abstractions must be earned. Try having your students reread the second paragraph (the first part of which is quoted above) and underline or circle any abstract word or description in the paragraph. Make a list of these on the board; students will root out a few words such as *necessity* or *habits*. Then ask them to count the number of concrete nouns in the passage and make a comparison. If you really want to drive the point home, try this exercise: Hand out or read a poem from one of the more flowery greeting cards to your students and have them circle abstractions in that poem. You'll likely get a list that includes words such as *love, peace, forever, joy, heart,* and that worst of all abstractions, *soul.* Discuss the effects of these two pieces of writing. Which one communicates a clearer picture? Which one leaves your students with a more immediate and personal feeling? Which one is better writing?

There is one abstraction in the second paragraph that denotes a major concept—it appears in a sentence just after the excerpt included above:

> Kiowa, a devout Baptist, carried an illustrated New Testament that had been presented to him by his father, who taught Sunday school in Oklahoma City, Okla-

> homa. As a hedge against bad times, however, Kiowa
> also carried his grandmother's distrust of the white man,
> his grandfather's old hunting hatchet. (3)

"Distrust" is a major abstract concept, but it appears here sandwiched between concrete details. How would the entire paragraph convey meaning differently, we ask our classes, if it began, "Kiowa was very distrustful of the white man"? Take this as an opportunity to discuss how authors "earn" their right to use abstractions and when those abstract concepts might be most valuable.

◆ *Selection of detail.* Henry Dobbins, a character who appears in this paragraph for the first time, carries "extra rations." O'Brien could have quit with that phrase, but he doesn't— instead, he tells us that Dobbins "was especially fond of canned peaches." That, too, could have become the stopping place, but we then also learn that these are peaches "in heavy syrup." Ask your students to find other such details in the story, and then discuss the effect of such details. Are any of them dispensable? Are all of them dispensable?

◆ *Juxtaposition of ideas.* Kiowa carries both a New Testament and weaponry; Ted Lavender carries a poncho that we are first told is useful as "a raincoat or groundsheet or makeshift tent" but then is in fact used to carry his dead body after he is shot. Have your students find other such juxtapositions in the story between the commonplace items and the implements of war that soldiers must carry. Note that O'Brien spends most of the story listing actual objects that soldiers carried in Vietnam, but that he juxtaposes those items, later in the story, with the other things soldiers carry: "They carried their own lives" (15), the narrator states in the middle of the story, and later tells us, "They carried their reputations. They carried the soldier's greatest fear, which was the fear of blushing" (21).

Writing

"The Things They Carried," as a writing prompt, almost assigns itself. The story works especially well to introduce the list poem, in which students simply list items they carry, paying attention to rhythm and detail. Remind students of the need to earn abstractions, the importance of specific detail and imagery, and the value of juxtaposition. Encourage them not to rhyme, since rhyme will probably distract them from saying what they most want to say, but to pay attention to the sound of the language itself.

This is a good time, too, to encourage students to make decisions about truth. Does every item in the poem have to be real? What best accomplishes the overall characterization or meaning of the poem? Where do their lives intersect with their art?

When our own eleventh- and twelfth-grade students write in response to this story each year, one common element quickly becomes apparent—while many of those in our school (and perhaps many teenagers in general) carry similar objects with them on a daily basis, the implications, suggestions, and connections those objects create vary wildly. Take, for instance, these samples from one group of student writers:

The Things I Carry

The things I carry:
A wallet, keys, chap-stick, a phone, Rolaids;
Not much, just to get me through the day.
Those things stay the same.
My wallet: an assortment of collected cards,

my ID, my ATM card, my Exxon card;
Three dollars (soon to be two),
Canadian money, old receipts, things I'm too lazy to throw away.
My keys, just two keys: a house and a car
with the beeper thing, I guess I'd call it a remote.

My chap-stick; I never need it unless I don't have it with me.
A phone: so I can know what I'm doing, without it I'd probably
    be lost (literally).
Rolaids: Heartburn's a pain.

Today I carry a white Abercrombie and Fitch shirt,
khaki pants, and wallabies.
Depending on what day it is, I can be seen with a laptop
and a couple of books at my side.

I carry with me the carelessness
that I have decided to adopt,
my ambitions, and my fears.
I carry friendship.
The weight of each of these is undetermined,
but they do not weigh me down.

—*Jared Herring*

Things I Carry

The necessary—
Books, nourishment, keys, glasses—
(all used or not, though my mom likes to think I did—
use them, that is)

The desired—
Music, photos, candy, memories
(all used, though my teachers like to think I didn't—
use them, that is)

jumbled together in my bag
(weighing two pounds or so)

Carrying my day
(in the form of a to-do list)

I can periodically sort through my stuff—
My food, my happiness, my relationships, my homework—
Before arrival at any given destination

At any given moment.

Knowing my mom left me cereal out of routine—
I persist in carrying it as
kindness

—*Sarah Ray*

The next poem balances abstraction with one or two important physical details:

I carry a jacket or a coat for protection
For protection from the world
Or to hide from the world and what is inside
Or to hide the truth and the lies
Depending on the weather
I carry my feeling, my emotions, my personality, and my thoughts
There are a lot of things I carry
But there are also things that carry me
My life carries me
It gives me hope and it gives me the will
Because of my life I am who I am
I am who I am because of the things I carry

—*Rhonda Spight*

O'Brien, in his description of soldiers, has also offered a strategy for teenage writers that students not only enjoy but also need—
the opportunity to explore how the physical objects that we choose
to make our own reflect internal motivations and enthusiasms.
Life and art intersect in the connection of the physical to the abstract, of description to reflection.

After the War

It may be that for some soldiers the war never ends. All of O'Brien's work, to some degree, involves memories of Vietnam. It's just as clear, though, that *The Things They Carried* marked a change in the novelist's work; the stories he has told since 1990 have focused on life after the war more than on life during the war. The characters that populate these stories—a failed politician, a veteran at a high school reunion, a narcissistic college professor—often grapple with memories of the war years, but they also face the challenges of daily life in American society. Here, for instance, is how O'Brien himself described the difference between his 1998 novel *Tomcat in Love* and his earlier work:

> Granted, the form of my novel is comedic. But at the same time that humor is rooted in the often painful realities of human experience. . . . [A]lthough *Tomcat in Love* is in one respect a departure for me—I wanted to write a funny book—it is no departure at all in the larger thematic sense. After all these years as a writer, I am still snagged by the same old obsessions: the things we do to win love, the things we will do to keep love, to love ourselves. (O'Brien, "An Interview with Tim O'Brien")

And, again, in *Ploughshares,* his own comparison of recent writing to his early novels: "The emotions in war and in our ordinary lives are, if not identical, damn similar" (Lee 196).

O'Brien's work continues to convert the personal past into fiction, to explore the tenuous connection between the truths of history and the truths of feeling and meaning—to exist at the intersection of life and art.

2 A True Story That Never Happened

▪ ▪

> *Absolute occurrence is irrelevant. A thing may happen and be*
> *a total lie; another thing may not happen and be truer than*
> *the truth.* (The Things They Carried 83)

Ask your students what *The Things They Carried* is about, and chances are the words *Vietnam*, *soldier*, and *war* will make it into their first few sentences. How would they react if you were to respond to their answers by telling them that none of the stories are about the Vietnam War, that all of the stories in the book are about the fine balance between truth and fact and why we tell stories? In the end, Tim O'Brien isn't examining the politics of the Vietnam War, the purpose of any war, or the nature of life and death. What O'Brien is trying to divine in this novel is why we tell stories and what purpose those stories—completely biased, subjective reports of events—serve in our lives. Central to this question is the idea that truth and fact might not be the same thing.

Lying gets a bad rap, we tell our students. We lie when we rationalize selfish behavior or pretend to be surprised when being told of a secret we've clandestinely known for months. What's more, we ask to be lied to on a regular basis. Every time we turn on the TV to watch a drama or comedy or go to the movies to see the latest blockbuster, or each time we open up a novel, we know the story is either completely or at least partially made up, and we like that. We enter into an agreement with the storyteller: as long as he or she doesn't break the contract of telling believable and entertaining lies, we will believe. This contract between creator and audience—the suspension of disbelief—is a key component of storytelling.

Of course, we don't want to advocate lying at *any* time. More than likely, you've taken a moment to discuss cheating and plagiarism with your students. Additionally, each of us can point to a time when we have been hurt by a deception. But at the same time, most of us have been moved by a story that was completely fabricated, and sometimes the fabrication moves us even more than a historically "factual" retelling of events may have done.

Blurring the Line

An in-depth look at a key story from *The Things They Carried*, "How to Tell a True War Story," follows later in this chapter, but one might use many sections of the novel to jump-start discussions about blurring this line between truth and fiction. For instance:

- We start a general exploration of the issue by asking students to tell a true story about themselves or their families. We ask them for personal stories, especially those that feed the students' or their families' identities:

    - Their earliest memories of their mothers

    - When their parents or grandparents met

    - When their families came to this country or this city

    - Their first days at new schools

- Their first experiences driving

- A story their families tell about themselves

This assignment starts as a discussion, but we like to ask students first to write down everything they know about the story without anyone else's input. They then ask others involved (such as parents or grandparents) to tell the same story with as much detail as possible. (This works better with some stories than with others.) In instances such as the parents' first meeting, the students ask both of the parents—separately—for their stories. When the students return with the stories and note the inevitable discrepancies, we discuss whether one is more or less "true" than the other. This discussion in turn leads to a discussion of subjectivity and memory. When does the truth stop being the truth in recounting events? If you tell a story that happened to you, but you say it happened when you were twelve and it actually happened when you were ten, are you lying? Is it no longer true?

▦ Another good place to start the discussion about blurring the line between fiction and nonfiction (after students have read at least one of the stories) is inside the book's covers but before we reach the text. Turn to the title page and you'll see a subtitle: *A Work of Fiction by Tim O'Brien*. The dedication page reads: "This book is lovingly dedicated to the men of Alpha Company, and in particular to Jimmy Cross, Norman Bowker, Rat Kiley, Mitchell Sanders, Henry Dobbins, and Kiowa." These are the names of the characters in the book. Is he dedicating this book to characters that he himself created? Were they real people who he is lying about? And, more to the point, how does this gray area make you as a reader feel about the veracity of the rest of the story? (In fact, the characters are just that—fictional characters. It's possible to find O'Brien's own explanation for this choice of dedication, in which he suggests that, when one lives with fictional characters for so long, they take on a sort of life. But we prefer to have students muse about the reasons for the dedication before letting them in on the secret.)

Before the story begins, O'Brien includes an epigraph from *John Ransom's Andersonville Diary* that seems to avow the "truthfulness" of the whole work. One question for students: how does this epigraph change the way you think of the novel before reading it and after?

- The blurring of the line between fact and fiction isn't just a concern of the author and the narrator—it's the central concern of the characters themselves. It shows up in the first paragraph of "The Things They Carried" as Lieutenant Cross struggles between what he wishes to be true about Martha, the girl in a picture he carries with him, and what he knows is true. He prefers the fiction at the beginning of the story, but by the end he resigns himself to turning his back on the fiction. Cross isn't trying to forget the fiction; he's just trying to survive. He feels that his dreaming of the girl has led to the death of one of his men. Not all the characters reject fiction or fantasy, though; each one comes to his own conclusion. Consider, for instance, O'Brien's description of Rat Kiley at the beginning of the story "Sweetheart of the Song Tra Bong," in which he tells us that "It wasn't a question of deceit" when Rat augmented stories; rather, "he wanted to heat up the truth, to make it burn so hot that you would feel exactly what he felt" (89). Try giving students a list of characters after they've read most of the stories and ask them to describe in a single sentence how each feels about truth and fiction.

- In "On the Rainy River," a story that flashes back to O'Brien's life before the war, the main character finds himself just a few feet from the Canadian border, literally on the edge of a huge decision: should he follow his draft orders or flee the country? In his real life, O'Brien didn't actually try to go to Canada the summer he graduated and was to report to active duty, nor did he go to the river; he has said he spent the summer playing golf and worrying. Emotionally, though, he was on that river. There is no suspense to showing a young man on the putting green, giving himself an ulcer. Here, we ask the students to refer back to any nonfiction stories they've written and to rewrite one in a setting that heightens whatever meaning they think the story has. We ask them to falsify a story to make it feel more true.

Metafiction

One of the major elements of *The Things They Carried* that contributes to the blurring of the line between (as O'Brien writes in the story "Good Form") "story-truth" and "happening-truth" is metafiction. Although many different styles can come under the broad heading of *metafiction*, the term essentially refers to storytelling about storytelling, exploring the value of experience, the malleability of memory, and the differences between fiction and reality.

Several times in the book, O'Brien the narrator stops to examine how and why he is telling these stories. In fact, at least seven of the twenty-two stories in the novel contain some metafictional approach, and some, like the chapter "Notes," are entirely reflections on earlier stories from the novel. The trick? Even those essayish chapters such as "Notes" contain fictions. Nonetheless, at the heart of O'Brien the author's intentions (as well as O'Brien the narrator's necessary self-exploration) in *The Things They Carried* is the idea that it is important to reflect on the stories we tell and on how and why we tell them. Interestingly,

O'Brien allows one of his own characters, Mitchell Sanders, to criticize this approach, but then uses Rat Kiley to offer his defense:

> [A]ll that matters is the raw material, the stuff itself, and you can't clutter it up with your own half-baked commentary. That just breaks the spell. It destroys the magic. What you have to do, Sanders said, is trust your own story. Get the hell out of the way and let it tell itself.
> But Rat Kiley couldn't help it. He wanted to bracket the full range of meaning. (106)

We use this passage to begin a discussion of metafiction in *The Things They Carried*. To what extent does O'Brien "destroy the magic"? Does he ever get out of the way of his own stories? What does he mean by suggesting that metafiction can "bracket the full range of meaning," and how does this work in the novel as a whole?

One of the first places O'Brien enters the world of metafiction is in the story "Spin," where he wishes that his stories could be labeled "peace stories." Then he gives us these paragraphs:

> Here's a quick peace story:
> A guy goes AWOL. Shacks up in Danang with a Red Cross nurse. It's a great time—the nurse loves him to death—the guy gets whatever he wants whenever he wants it. The war's over, he thinks. Just nookie and new angles. But then one day he rejoins his unit in the bush. Can't wait to get back into action. Finally one of his buddies asks what happened with the nurse, why so hot for combat, and the guy says, "All that peace, man, it felt so good it *hurt*. I want to hurt it *back*." (35)

And then we learn that Mitchell Sanders told that story to the narrator and that he made most of it up. What follows in "Spin" is a series of quick vignettes, varying between the comic, the grotesque, and the mundane, some only single phrases, until O'Brien ends the chapter:

> Forty-three years old, and the war occurred half a lifetime ago, and yet the remembering makes it now. And sometimes remembering will lead to a story, which makes it forever. That's what stories are for. Stories are for joining the past to the future. Stories are for those late hours in the night when you can't remember how you got from where you were to where you are. Stories are for eternity, when memory is erased, where there is nothing to remember except the story. (38)

Compare this to the last paragraph of the last story, "The Lives of the Dead," as the writer dreams of Linda, a little girl he's been remembering:

> And then it becomes 1990. I'm forty-three years old, and a writer now, still dreaming Linda alive in exactly the same way. She's not the embodied Linda; she's mostly made up, with a new identity and a new name, like the man who never was. Her real name doesn't matter. . . . I'm skimming across the surface of my own history, moving fast, riding the melt beneath the blades, doing loops and spins, and when I take a high leap into the dark and come down thirty years later, I realize it is as Tim trying to save Timmy's life with a story. (245–46)

So the framework of the entire book is one in which a writer tells his readers stories—made-up stories—and then tells us why he's telling us those stories: to reveal emotional truth.

O'Brien pauses in the telling of his stories several other times either to wonder if he is telling the stories correctly or to explain that he is fabricating stories. In some sections, he tells a story and then retells it in a way that alters the original story. A good example of this is "How to Tell a True War Story." This story actually contains several stories, with comments from the author/narrator about each. Consider this brief outline of the chapter's components:

I. O'Brien describes Rat Kiley's letter about his dead friend Curt Lemon to Lemon's sister. In this story, Rat is clearly trying to express his raw emotions about how important Lemon was to him, and his honesty is painful. In fact, usually at least one student will remark that these aren't the stories Rat should be writing to the sister. It relates to what the narrator says later about obscenity.

II. We hear the story of how Lemon died. There's not much reflection here, but the narrator returns to this story a little later.

III. Mitchell Sanders tells the story about the listening patrol. In this story, the patrol worries about how they could possibly tell the truth about what they heard to people who weren't there. Ultimately they decide they can't. It's a story Mitchell stops in the middle of to tell the narrator that he won't believe it "[b]ecause it happened. Because every word is absolutely dead-on true" (74).

Sometimes we teach this story out of the order listed in the course syllabus, even in the middle of studying another work entirely, when students begin to complain that they can't "relate" to fiction because it isn't "real." Mitchell's story calls the veracity of any story into question. So many kids say about stories they like: "That stuff really happens" or "I know someone who is just like that." We often have this discussion with classes when studying *The Catcher in the Rye*; students claim they "relate" to Holden even though they've never been to New York City or dropped out of school or ended up in a mental asylum. But why Holden (who, incidentally, is also concerned about believability—note how often he implores us to believe him, that he's telling us what "really" happened) and not, say, Hamlet or Homer?

Mitchell comes back after telling the fantastical story of the listening patrol and says he had to make some of it up. We also like to teach this short passage just after a class reads a story that they think imparts some direct and facile lesson the writer is trying to teach, such as "always tell the truth" or "never judge a book by its cover." The moral of Mitchell's story is the "quiet" (77)—which isn't defined, perhaps harkening back to his earlier assertion that there isn't a moral at all. The narrator wavers back and forth between moral ambiguities and admits later that true war stories are contradictory.

IV. The narrator then retells the story about Lemon and then Rat killing the water buffalo. We ask students if they think this was the story the narrator was hesitating to tell originally and whether the reason he seems to be doubling back over his stories might be because he didn't want to tell this one.

V. The narrator tells Lemon's story again . . .

VI. and then he tells it again . . .

VII. and then he tells us it was all made up.

Along with these major sections, we hear O'Brien's commentary on the nature of war stories, of war, and of stories. A discussion about "How to Tell a True War Story" can go in several different directions:

- How does it affect our reading when the narrator stops, wonders about how to tell a story, and then retells it, changing the details bit by bit? We are left to feel that it is less factual, but has it become less true? What used to be hard facts are now malleable details—why?

- When O'Brien addresses the reader directly and says, "[t]his is true" (67), or, as in "On the Rainy River" when he says, "This is one story I've never told before" (39), the intimacy serves to draw the reader in. When we as audience feel like the author's confidant, we buy into the conceit. It's like sharing a secret. When a character does this, the effect is the same. But then, when the character or narrator tells a story again and again, slightly or completely differently, at what point does it become a fabrication? Is there a point at which we feel manipulated or betrayed by the narrator or characters?

- The author tells us, seven stories into the book and in the same story that starts with "This is true," that everything in the book is made up, a sentiment he repeats several times throughout the novel. In addition, the story "Good Form" returns to the concept that everything in the book is true and fabricated at the same time. Can an idea exist as both a truth and a fabrication? Many of us don't tolerate this concept in the realms of politics or religion, nor is it acceptable in an interpretation of school rules. Why should we tolerate it in fiction?

- When someone is telling you a story and he or she says, "This part is true," how does that reflect on the reliability of the storyteller? Are we supposed to think that all the other chapters or stories *aren't* true because no one has weighed in with that caveat?

(One might be reminded of Gertrude's famous observation, "The lady protests too much, methinks"). And what does it mean that the author is doing this in the midst of a book that has as its subtitle "A Work of Fiction"?

■ Tim O'Brien the character plays a role in some of the chapters but not all of them. Is that to imply that he witnesses some of what goes on in the book but not all of it? Does it make the narrator more or less reliable that he never tells us the answer to this question?

One effect of metafiction is to undo everything the author has attempted to create, because the author is admitting that he is manipulating the reader, rearranging facts, leaving out what did happen and adding in things that didn't. He's lying in order to tell the truth, he would argue, and this idea serves as a pathway to powerful discussions and writing exercises. We often ask students to create a lie that tells us the truth. A few ideas:

■ Discuss and practice writing dialogue with students. O'Brien admits freely that his first work, *If I Die in a Combat Zone*, which is usually billed as nonfiction, contains fabricated dialogue that is true to his memory but perhaps not to fact—after all, what soldier takes notes on everything his comrades *actually* say? Ask students to remember a real event and reconstruct the dialogue as it might have been. This might even be a good time to introduce the concept of irony; students can try having a character mean something other than he or she says only through dialogue.

■ After students compile family histories such as those mentioned earlier in this chapter, have them write the story of, say, how their parents or grandparents met—a fiction based on truth.

▨ A more specific exercise to ease students into the idea of blurring the line between fact and fiction is to have them write about an actual event from their own lives but also require them to add objects or aspects of your design: a pair of pink socks, a scene in a kitchen, a crazy relative who shows up uninvited, a diary entry, etc.

In the following excerpt from one student's short story, for instance, the narrator recalls the death of a younger sibling many years earlier. This story, while based on a real event from the author's life, is recounted here through the lens of memory and style; the author also makes a conscious decision to set the scene in a fictional encounter between the narrator and her psychiatrist:

> The painful pulling-of-teeth feeling is coming back, my stomach is rising up to the top of my throat, but I know I have to get it out: I have to tell someone. I have to get rid of the secret insecurities that haunt me at every playground, swimming pool, and front yard.
>
> "I wanted to play with him, so I walked into his room to wake him up from his afternoon nap. When I didn't see him, I ran and told my parents who were sitting in their room. They ran past me, my mom searching under blankets in his crib, and then out the door they went. I asked myself, should I go help? Why was the door unlocked? Why did he go outside?" My sentences short, immature and my voice unstable. "I sat, screaming, alone in the house, knowing deep down something was terribly wrong. My neighbor came inside and pulled me by the arm to the dock, and I saw him. I saw two people who used to be my parents standing over a boy who use to be my brother. What I left on that dock was my childhood and every reason to ever think life was going to be the same. Time stopped for him: eighteen-months old, never a day older."

> "No wonder you are such a mother-figure—very control-ling." The stoic woman now looks up from her yellow pad. "You feel like you have to protect everything and everyone."
>
> —*Mary Beth Epps*

What struck us about this story was that by framing the subject as a fiction, Mary Beth not only managed to explore a painful topic in her writing, but she also managed to reflect on her own character and reactions. Fabricated dialogue allowed her to see the true consequences of the events she writes about.

Literary and Cultural Examples of Blurring the Line That Can Lead to Discussion

There never seems to be a shortage of people in our culture who play with their own stories. Look at Eminem. He's born Marshall Mathers, renames himself Eminem, raps stories from the perspective of his alter ego Slim Shady about things he has done or imagines doing in his own life, then makes the semiautobiographical movie *8 Mile*. He often talks about violence in terms of how he feels rather than what he has done. Stephen King has published under a pseudonym, Andy Kaufman played characters without ever revealing to the audience that they were characters, Paul Auster writes stories in which there are characters named Paul Auster—examples like these can be great starting points for further discussion of *The Things They Carried*.

As part of that discussion, we often bring up cultural examples of "liars" in order to discuss how we should deal with them. It might start with a little homework. Give each student one or two names to look up; here are just a few we have read about in the last year: James Frey, JT LeRoy, Nasdijj, Helen Darville, Kaavya Viswanathan, Leon Carmen, Augusten Burroughs, Jayson Blair,

Stephen Glass, Rigoberta Menchu. In the age of Google and Wikipedia, it is quite simple to look these things up. (In fact, Wikipedia itself offers an interesting discussion point about how we tell history. Usually we rely on scholars, but anyone can make an entry on Wikipedia. There are even a few cases in which entries have been made that were purposely incorrect in order to attack someone.)

People on the previous list have plagiarized fiction, fabricated works of journalism, or lied about their pasts. When the students bring back their research and share it with the group, ask how we should judge such figures. Do we judge them all by the same standards? Do we then apply those standards to an author like O'Brien? Can we come to an agreement about which kinds of fictionalization are acceptable and which aren't?

In addition to all the writers who seem to have blurred the line between fact and fiction or who have lied to tap in to our need to hear true stories, there are other aspects of our popular culture that deal with gray areas between reality and fantasy:

- Movies that have the tagline "based on a true story" (also, "based on real events")

- Reenactments on "true crime" shows

- Reality television

Each of these examples takes something that is factual and alters it for our entertainment (or, in the case of reality television, uses untrained amateurs to perform in an ostensibly unscripted scene). How far away is such entertainment from reality? What definition of *reality* do we apply to the stories with which we surround ourselves? How does that definition affect the way we read?

3 Writing from Models

> *You take your material where you find it, which is in your life, at the intersection of past and present. The memory-traffic feeds into a rotary up on your head, where it goes in circles for a while, then pretty soon imagination flows in and the traffic merges and shoots off down a thousand different streets.* (The Things They Carried 34–35)

Students usually get a kick out of T. S. Eliot's famous maxim about where writers get their inspiration: "Immature poets," he once wrote, "imitate; mature poets steal." It's a clever line, but we've also found it bears some discussion; after all, we don't want students to think we're advocating plagiarism. Here's how such a discussion might go:

TEACHER: So, if you're a poet, who are you going to steal *from*?

MARCUS: Really rich people!

TEACHER: Ha-ha . . .

MARCUS: Okay, right, he's talking about other poets.

JESSICA: Or other writers in general. Like Shakespeare or someone.

TEACHER: Okay, so the next question is, *what* are you going to steal? Are you just going to put your name on act 1 of *Hamlet* and try to sell it to a publisher? Is that what Eliot means?

HECTOR: I think he's talking about just certain lines or phrases. Like that Robert Frost poem we read with the Shakespeare line in the title.

TEACHER: You're talking about "Out, Out."

HECTOR: Right. It just makes it better because of the references.

MICHELLE: Allusions.

TEACHER: Right, but using allusions is just sort of borrowing, isn't it? Because you're not really trying to make anyone think you wrote the line yourself; in fact, a good allusion only works if your reader knows exactly where it comes from. Isn't the idea of stealing *not* to get caught?

JESSICA: Gee, sounds like you have a lot of experience with theft. . . .

TEACHER: As a writer, sure. Look, when I write, I keep a big stack of books beside my computer, and if I ever get stuck, I pick up one of those books at random, open it up to a random page, and read a sentence or paragraph. Then I keep writing, but I don't use the words I just read. So why does that help me?

MARCUS: I get it. It's like you just need to see how some other writer started a sentence or something.

MICHELLE: Like when we do peer editing with our essays. Sometimes I just like to see how someone else starts their essay off differently from me.

TEACHER: Good. So what are we stealing, then?

MICHELLE: Just sort of a way of writing, I guess.

JIM: It's like, style and sentence structure.

MICHELLE: That's what I meant. But you could even steal more than a sentence. You could, like, steal a whole way of writing a story with flashbacks or something.

MARCUS: But isn't that just imitating?

JESSICA: Like he said, not if you don't get caught. . . .

And what the heck, as long as we're headed in this direction, imagine the discussion continuing like this:

TEACHER: Absolutely. Take this sample class conversation, for instance. I included it partly because I saw how effective such a sample discussion was in the first three books in this series by Carol Jago—I'm pretty much "stealing" from her right now.

MICHELLE: But we had a real conversation just like this in class! Now you're claiming that everything I'm saying right now is just made up?

TEACHER: Right.

MICHELLE: But I really said things like this.

TEACHER: Exactly. The content is real, but the structure is based on an effective convention I learned from someone else. But this discussion fits right in, doesn't it? Really makes my point.

What's the teacher's point? Just this: in the writing classroom, emulation is an effective tool for addressing not only what students write about but also how they write. The combination of the two—content and style—is what leads to successful student writing, and Tim O'Brien is as good a model for both aspects of the craft as any writer we know.

To help students focus on each of these areas and to minimize the natural tendency to rewrite an author's work instead of just emulating it, we separate writing assignments that follow a reading of O'Brien's work in this way: we assign students to write prose that imitates the style and structure, but not the content, of stories from the novels and to write poetry that bounces off the subject matter, but not necessarily the style, of those stories.

Take, for instance, the following model assignments for prose and poetry.

Prose

Almost none of the students we have taught has been directly involved in an actual war (several have had close relatives who have fought or died in wars, and some international students have survived major conflict). Many of those students, on the other hand—perhaps all—have encountered personal tragedy or suffering, and all have memories and experiences that are worth writing about. Often, in fact, the most frequent complaint of students in writing classes—"Nothing interesting has happened to me"—could really be translated into this statement: "I don't know how to write about the things that have happened to me in an interesting way."

The third story in *The Things They Carried,* like the title story, is structured in a nonlinear fashion that we've found particularly effective for high school writers. A collection of vignettes, "Spin" is made up of anecdotes, memories, and brief commentary. Unlike the standard short story model many students are taught, in which there must be a beginning, middle, and end or rising and falling action, O'Brien creates a patchwork of moments such as this one:

> I remember Norman Bowker and Henry Dobbins playing checkers every evening before dark. It was a ritual for them. They would dig a foxhole and get the board out and play long, silent games as the sky went from pink to purple. The rest of us would sometimes stop by to watch. There was something restful about it, something orderly and reassuring. There were red checkers and black checkers. The playing field was laid out in a strict grid, no tunnels or mountains or jungles. You knew where you stood. You knew the score. The pieces were out on the board, the enemy was visible, you could watch the tactics unfolding into larger strategies. There was a winner and a loser. There were rules. (32)

This story is short enough to read aloud in less than a class period, with each student reading one paragraph or section (there are eighteen short sections in all). After such a reading, we ask students to list some of the strategies O'Brien uses to give the reader a sense of his experience. Here's a sample list from one class:

- Short, seemingly unrelated stories or anecdotes on a similar topic.

- Occasional sentences of commentary about the meaning of the story, but nothing heavy-handed (note the last sentences of the preceding example, which make the checker game metaphorical without ever stating outright that it's a metaphor).

- Lots of physical details—these are stories, not philosophy.

- Single-sentence paragraphs with very short sentences at the start or end of the sections.

- Intentional sentence fragments.

- Parallel openings: several of the sections start with "I remember," for instance. In fact, there are many of examples of repetition and parallelism throughout the story.

This isn't a formula, and it isn't always a successful approach for student writers. But for students who have trouble sustaining their focus while writing a long piece, for students who are grappling with a broad theme or topic, or for students who simply roll their eyes at the idea of writing a short story, this approach can be not just helpful but also invigorating.

Nonetheless, it was natural to be taken aback when one student asked, "Can I write my college essay like that?" Could she? Sure. Why not? For years, we've struggled to help students with the mandatory essay on college applications, to guide them in their writing without manipulating their writing or writing for them. For these students, the personal essay suddenly means something, and the pressure is on—the result of which is often a mishmash of triteness and abstraction. The students try so hard to say something that they wind up saying nothing at all.

Enter O'Brien. Using the list of strategies above and a standard "tell us who you are in five hundred words or less" prompt, several of our students that year produced excellent personal statements, and we've suggested nonlinear structure as a possibility ever since. Observe how one student, Nadia, explored her own identity in this nonlinear form:

> What defines "Nadia"? Is it that I'm full-blooded Egyptian and full-brained American, Muslim and Christian, 5-foot-7-and-a-half-inches with unmanageable hair and half-painted fingernails? Or is it my endless competitiveness, insatiable curiosity and regretful indifference, knowledge, intelligence, and also a lack thereof, encapsulated in a still-teenage girl of seventeen?
>
> I'm 3.4% of the American population—an INFP (Introverted, Intuitive, Feeling, and Perceptive)—who likes abstraction and perfection, believes in the fluidity of deadlines, bores easily, and is just as easily fascinated. INFPs are modern bra-burners, impassioned and liberal, meaning-seekers, truth-lovers. I'm

your average teenager, but then again, I'm not—because I don't want to be. I'm nature and I'm nurture, a product of my blood-line and a creation of my own desire. I fear the absolute, yet—or because—I know it all too well.

A story: When I was ten years old, my family went on a trip to Italy. I remember standing in awe of the masterpieces of Florence, but I cannot remember the artwork. Maybe, as a child, I knew the significance of the canvases before me and was awed by the label "masterpiece" itself rather than any particular paint-ing. What I do remember is sitting up late one night, giggling girlishly with my little sister Nora about the phrase "eau de toilette," of course mistaking the word "toilette" for toilet in my callow erudition, yet also primitively understanding the irony in naming a smell-good product for something so noto-rious for smelling so bad. The next day, after a compromise over who would ride in the back of the station wagon, our car went out of control, and the family crashed; days later, Nora died.

I'm not a very good storyteller. I omit details, rush through painful parts, try to hide the sensitive ones. At ten years old, I was embarrassed to cry. Today, at seventeen, I struggle with feeling continually embarrassed for telling—and for not tell-ing—the story. Embarrassed because I feel like I exploit her memory in the telling, I feel guilty when parts become routine, when I can say the words without crying, and maybe some-times without feeling. Embarrassed also because I feel like I tarnish her memory by locking it up in a closet, right across from my own, and guilty for clearing out her shelves to make room for my own soccer gear—as if I cared about soccer more than her. Embarrassed to think that people will read this, will read it in broad daylight after a cup of coffee, and oh, what will they think of me? Guilty every time I look at my new little sister, Lilah, and call her Nora; and think: they have the same hair, the same smile, the same cute, pudgy knees, the same innocence. And think: they have the same soul. And think: you don't know what you're talking about.

I may not know what I'm talking about.

Another story: Last week, out on the soccer field, I got tackled. Hard. And another girl beat me. When I got up, I was angry, and I set out to hit her back.

In this scenario, you feel no pity for me, there are no euphemisms, no touchy subjects, nothing uncomfortable to face, no DEATH. I was not the sensitive person I've described myself to be, but a vengeful one, indulging in all the same feelings that exist intrinsically, though often subdued, in each and every one of us, and there I was, openly anxious to gratify my own vendetta at the expense of another. Does that make me any less attractive as a person?

No. It makes me real.

I wonder if I'm really myself, and I see the paradox there. I'm daddy's little girl and too grown up for my mom at the same time. I'm a closet rebel and a banner-toting liberal. I'm Bloomingdale's and thrift stores; the suburbs of Memphis, Tennessee; the sands of Memphis, Egypt. I fear being just one person. Redundant and brand-spanking-new, I'm my older brother's disciple, part of Nora's spirit, and my two younger siblings' example. I'm a girl with questions, inquisitiveness, and thirst, who fights to be on the front page, but understands the importance of teamwork. And I try.

I'm not a contradiction—I'm a compilation. All people are.
—*Nadia Gaber*

We wouldn't immediately think of O'Brien upon reading this essay, but the influence is there: in the fragments, the structure, the details, the single sentence paragraphs, the repetition. Nadia stole, but she also took what she stole and made it absolutely her own (and it worked, by the way—Nadia was accepted to Harvard).

Major Life Decisions
One of the most astounding moments in any O'Brien story occurs in the last line of "On the Rainy River," when the narrator, having reached the Canadian border, considers all of those whom

he would disappoint if he fled the draft and offers us this paradox: "I was a coward. I went to the war."

To begin our study of this story, we discuss the final line with the class, define the word *paradox*, and then ask the students to write a paradoxical sentence of their own, imitating O'Brien's as closely as they wish. Often, we have students copy these statements in marker onto construction paper sheets, which we then tape (anonymously) to the board. The statements themselves, especially when there are several to choose from, suggest and inspire stories and poems. Imagine for yourself what explanations might lead to conclusions such as:

"I'm not a good student. I do my homework every day."

"It isn't hard to make good grades. All you have to do is never read a book."

"My parents really love each other. That's why they're divorced."

Of course, the focus of the story is a major life decision—a decision with more at stake than some others, perhaps, but a decision that bears some resemblance to those all of us must make at some point. For O'Brien, the *process* of making the decision becomes a focal point. Observe the details he uses to re-create his interior reaction to being drafted:

At some point in mid-July I began thinking seriously about Canada. The border lay a few hundred miles north, an eight-hour drive. Both my conscience and my instincts were telling me to make a break for it, just take off and run like hell and never stop. In the beginning the idea seemed purely abstract, the word Canada printing itself out in my head; but after a time I could see the particular shapes and images, the sorry details of my own future—a hotel room in Winnipeg, a battered old suitcase, my father's eyes as I tried to explain myself over the telephone. I could almost hear his voice, and my mother's. Run, I'd think. Then I'd think, Impossible. Then a second later I'd think, *Run*. (44)

Teenagers face tough choices all the time, and there isn't always one outcome that's clearly superior to another. Notice the way this student uses O'Brien's powerful line as a springboard for personal reflection; this paragraph comes from a personal essay about a school-sponsored field trip:

One of the guys that I hung out with was stupid. He decided to drink cough syrup diluted with water; it wasn't enough for him to just smoke cigarettes in his room. I was stupider. I let him. I was selfish. I fled his hotel room hoping to put all of the guilt behind me, guilt by association, by inaction. Arriving in my own room I was aloof and thought I had escaped any possible persecution; had this been the case I may never have had the opportunity for change. The trip chaperones came calling for me; they questioned me about the guy who had drunk the cough syrup. I was a coward; I stuck by my friend. I lied to them, telling them I knew nothing. The ruse failed, on the worst of all possible conditions—regretting my lying, failure to stop the guy, and self-centeredness—I confirmed that he indeed drank the syrup; I told them all that they had wanted to know. Every fear I had, justified and unjustified, came pouring out. Luckily for me there was someone more mature, more intelligent and more altruistic than I to listen to me. Retelling this portion of the tale becomes difficult because my thoughts seemed to pour out before they had even become fully assembled in my own mind. All I know for certain are my fears: I was afraid of retribution and anger from the guy that drank the syrup, but far more than that I was afraid that somehow my mother would become involved and she would associate me with people who go around drinking cough syrup for kicks.
—*Andrei Anghelescu*

Poetry

Personal Tragedies

The Things They Carried ends with a jolt: after twenty-one chapters that are set in or deal mostly with the war, the final story, "The Lives of the Dead," describes the narrator's reaction to a death of a nine-year-old girl, Linda, whom he knew as a boy. Though he knows Linda is sick, the young narrator, Timmy, remains in denial until he hears of the death from a classmate:

> . . . "All right," I finally said. "So will she get better now?"
>
> "Well, no," my mother said, "I don't think so." She stared at a spot behind my shoulder. "Sometimes people don't ever get better. They die sometimes."
>
> I shook my head.
>
> "Not Linda," I said.
>
> But on a September afternoon, during noon recess, Nick Veenhof came up to me on the school playground. "Your girlfriend," he said, "she kicked the bucket."
>
> At first I didn't understand.
>
> "She's dead," he said. "My mom told me at lunchtime. No lie, she actually kicked the goddang *bucket*."
>
> All I could do was nod. Somehow it didn't quite register. I turned away, glanced down at my hands for a second, then walked home without telling anyone. (237)

The realm of personal tragedy is both rich ground and dangerous territory for teenagers. Some of the rules here are absolute: there must be a measure of trust and respect between writers and readers, whether the audience is a sole teacher, a class of students, or the world at large. For all poems, but especially for poems such as these, we set some guidelines in class: the first comment must always be positive, students must treat others' words as if they were their own, and we give every poem the time and attention it deserves. Also, any teacher must be sure not to treat tragedy as currency rather than just another avenue for exploration; the student whose life has not been torn apart by misfortune shouldn't be made to feel that he or she has "nothing to write about," for instance.

O'Brien's work serves as a wonderful model for students who need to write about their own lives, be the focus death, divorce, or even a loss as common (but complex) as that of a pet, because stories such as "The Lives of the Dead" rest on physical detail and reactions that are realistic, not overly dramatic. Witness these two poems that came from the same class of students. The first is an attempt to capture the complex emotions of a mother's cancer:

> Darkened rooms
> malodorous with sterility,
> crumbly biscuits, granular,
> extra sweet Jell-o cubes,
> and monitors and wires
> lurking in corners
> and snaking up bed frames.
> Esurient patients dying (some literally)
> for nurturing of the health and soul.
> Neighbors processing
> in endless waves to our front door,
> Groaning under the weight of casseroles,
> barbeque, chicken noodle soup.
> My cheeks are permanently salted
> like the rims of discarded margarita glasses,
> The dogs know that mom
> is not to be trifled with. They don't jump up.
> No one treats me the same;
> they think I am delicate,
> Fragile, and about to break
> into waves of miserable sobbing.
> The house is quiet, dad looks harrowed,
> Dark circles envelope his eyes,

and he doesn't cry . . . ever.
Looking back,
I see that the cancer deadens and dulls
the usually vibrant
aspects of everyday existence.

—*Phoebe Fraser*

The following poem came from the same assignment, but this student decided to take a more humorous, and equally valid, approach:

(A personal tragedy)

Of course I suspected nothing.
But sure enough
And it wasn't just the red symbol for stop prohibiting me from
    departing

The pitter patter confirmed that the world was sad for my
    misfortune as well
My golden key
I inserted it into its home for a second time
And a third

VROOOM it yelled at me!
And together, my machine and my person drove
Until it decided it wanted to have a cigar

I saw the grey
I steered my machine to the right, into a lot
I opened the hood

Scalding hot fluorescent green ERUPTED
Terribles wafted past my nose
Like the tin man, the hot beast became frozen
For I had no oil

—*Mia Baer*

Both of these poems originated with assignments given during the study of O'Brien's works, but the products are quite different. In a classroom that creates a safe environment for young writers, both poems can be valued and enjoyed.

Living with War

Back in high school, our English teachers had us write poems about growing up in the nuclear age. Some of our childhood fears of nuclear war may seem outdated or limited now; today's students may view the cold war or threats of worldwide nuclear warfare as ancient history. Nonetheless, many of the themes of life during a time of war resonate as loudly today as they did during O'Brien's years in Vietnam. For some students, using the author's work as a springboard to reflect on the events that surround them now provides a way to explore issues of war and violence:

Chronological Fury

Face red
Like Arizona dirt
She doesn't watch the news anymore
Too much violence
A pitcher overflowing
Instead she sits by her window
Lacing string through her fingers
Repetitive as a skipped CD
She stares at the picture on the table
Surrounded by the bag of cough drops
Cherry-flavored
Crying thinking of the way it was
Bombs dropping people crying
She waits in the clubhouse

> For her mother who never came back
> Seconds lost then minutes and years
> —*Sarah Insch*

In one sense, O'Brien's subject matter is timeless—students today live with the realities of war just as those in previous generations did. Though some of the circumstances may differ, many of the underlying emotional responses remain the same.

4 The Simple Need to Talk

"I'd been writing sentences for three months, until a sentence came that lasted. Each of the sentences I had done before attracted me a little bit, but then I'd cast it aside after an hour or two and try another possibility. Like fishing. I don't know if I was fishing for tuna or carp or minnows. I had no idea what I was fishing for. I just wanted to fish for a little bit." (O'Brien, "A Conversation with Tim O'Brien")

In a lecture at Brown University, Tim O'Brien offered five guidelines for aspiring writers. The first: "Writing never gets easier. It gets harder. You can't repeat yourself." It's true, of course, that many writers (O'Brien included) revisit familiar territory—Vietnam, for instance—and that all good writers develop a toolbox of stylistic devices and approaches they may repeat and hone. But O'Brien's right; not only can't a writer repeat himself exactly, but also, for many writers, the more one learns about writing, the more one sees the difficulties and challenges of writing well.

We sometimes think one might substitute the word *teaching* for *writing* in O'Brien's aphorism. Experienced teachers repeat lessons, teach the same books again, teach the same subjects for more than one year. But great teachers are always on the lookout for new approaches, new practices, new ways to present material to students in a shifting culture.

Teaching students to write, however, means using models and accessing those devices and structures authors rely on as foundations for new stories. Teaching a work like *The Things They Carried* offers the chance to examine style at several levels; it's worth considering O'Brien's syntax, the structure within his stories and chapters, and even the structure of entire novels. In each case, there's a lesson for students both as readers and as writers.

O'Brien's other four rules, incidentally, are worth remembering as well. Among them are the admonitions to "use active verbs" and to avoid ridiculous similes, unintentional puns, and alliteration that makes sentences sound silly. As a final caveat, he offers his audience this observation: "A writer must, above all, write. . . . [A]s much as writing hurts, it carries with it, at times, content, satisfaction."

The satisfaction of reading Tim O'Brien's work arises from the multiple levels of artistry he brings to his craft, from the choice of a single word to the choices necessary to tie a two-hundred-page novel together, such as approaches to narrative framework, point of view, and chronological sequencing.

Within the Story: From Phrases to Paragraphs

Most writing teachers would agree: there's almost no literary concept so elusive, so hard to pin down, as the idea of a writer's "voice." What makes O'Brien's voice his own? The way he structures a sentence? The fact that he uses recurring images such as sunlight no matter what he's writing? The diction he provides for characters? Some combination of these aspects of his writing and more? It's tough to say, yet read an O'Brien novel and you know you're reading O'Brien. It's not just that he *doesn't* write like Dickens or Fitzgerald or Kerouac, it's that he *writes* like Tim O'Brien.

We can categorize and study some of the tools that make O'Brien's voice unique. We can even mimic some of them, incorporate them into our own voices. We can study how those tools help the writer convey his message and meaning. We can't reduce his style, his voice, to a simple list of techniques, however. Just as plot summaries can't replace a plot, a list of rhetorical strategies can't replace voice. But sometimes a close analysis of style can yield a greater understanding of and appreciation for that voice, and for both engaging students as readers and helping them to read closely for style, there's no better example than O'Brien's writing. For instance, take this passage, the opening of the second chapter of *The Nuclear Age*:

> When I was a kid, about Melinda's age, I converted my Ping-Pong table into a fallout shelter. Funny? Poignant? A nifty comment on the modern age? Well, let me tell you something. The year was 1958, and I was scared. Who knows how it started? Maybe it was all that CONELRAD stuff on the radio, tests on the Emergency Broadcast System, pictures of H-bombs in *Life* magazine, strontium 90 in the milk, the times in school when we'd crawl under our desks and cover our heads in practice for the real thing. Or maybe it was rooted deep inside me. In my own inherited fears, in the genes, in a coded conviction that the world wasn't safe for human life.
>
> Really, who knows?
>
> Whatever the sources, I was a frightened child. At night I'd toss around in bed for hours, battling the snagged sheets, and then when sleep finally came, sometimes close to dawn, my dreams would be clotted with sirens and melting ice caps and radioactive gleamings and ICBMS whining in the dark.
>
> I was a witness. I saw it happen. In dreams, in imagination, I watched the world end. (9)

Compare the tools O'Brien uses to create his narrator's voice here with those mentioned in the study of "How to Tell a True War Story" in the previous chapter and you'll start to see some similarities:

- Concrete, physical details

- Intentional sentence fragments

- Intentional short sentences alternating with longer sentences

- One-sentence paragraphs

- Rhetorical questions

You could also add some of the devices particular to this passage:

- Polysyndeton (the use of a conjunction several times in one sentence: "sirens and melting ice caps and radioactive gleamings")

- Metaphor ("battling the snagged sheets")

- Syntactical repetition for effect ("I was a witness. I saw it happen.")

- Allusion (in this case, to the details of a historical era: the cold war and the race for nuclear proliferation. O'Brien expects his readers to be familiar, for instance, with *Life* magazine and its context in American culture.)

There's a good bit to be learned from the close reading of such a passage, not the least of which is the terminology readers (and writers) use to study how a work is written. Here's an approach we use in our own classrooms:

- Divide the students into groups and give each group a passage from the work.

- Ask each group to list any interesting, unusual, or noticeable uses of language or syntax, whether or not the groups know what the device is called.

- Make a list on the board of all the devices found by all the groups (mark those found by more than one group).

- As the students point out the devices or tools, name them; this is a good opportunity to teach some terminology. (We might say, "It's great that you guys noticed the repetition of *and* in that sentence; that's technically called 'polysyndeton.'")

- Discuss the list as a class. What tools or devices appear in more than one passage? (Often, students will see devices in their own passages once other groups point them out in reference to their readings.) What common effect do those devices create? Can you begin to characterize the voice of the author through the analysis of recurring devices?

There's more to reading than simply listing devices and syntactical approaches, of course. The details and content of the passage are essential to creating the voice of this particular narrator. But O'Brien's own voice lurks in the style. That doesn't mean, however, that the author can't adapt the way he writes to suit the occasion. Notice this section—only part of one sentence, from the end of "On the Rainy River":

> All my aunts and uncles were there, and Abraham Lincoln, and Saint George, and a nine-year old girl named Linda who had died of a brain tumor back in fifth grade, and several members of the United States Senate, and a blind poet scribbling notes, and LBJ, and Huck Finn, and Abbie Hoffman, and all the dead soldiers back from the grave, and the many thousands who were later to die. (58)

More allusions, right? More polysyndeton, too. But what really stands out about this sentence, which continues for some time in this way, is how O'Brien uses an unusually long sentence—unusual especially in *The Things They Carried*—to capture the thought process of a stressed and morally uncertain young man making one of the most crucial decisions of his lifetime. There's a term for the effect the writer creates here: *stream of consciousness*—not a term we'd normally associate with this author. But O'Brien's telltale style reasserts itself with the next two paragraphs, the second of which is presented here in its entirety:

> I tried to will myself overboard. (59)

"Never forget the glorious sunset of a period," we once heard Tim O'Brien say in a lecture on the craft of writing. His meaning: don't forget that a short sentence can deliver as powerful a punch as a long one.

With O'Brien's penchant for brevity of syntax in mind, it's worth examining the writer's use of dialogue as well. Take, for example, this exchange between the narrator and his fictional daughter in the story "Field Trip":

> One morning in Saigon she'd asked what it was all about. "This whole war," she said, "why was everybody so mad at everybody else?"
>
> I shook my head. "They weren't mad, exactly. Some people wanted one thing, other people wanted another thing."
>
> "What did *you* want?"
>
> "Nothing," I said. "To stay alive."
>
> "That's all?"
>
> "Yes."
>
> Kathleen sighed. "Well, I don't get it. I mean, how come you were even here in the first place?" (*The Things They Carried* 183)

It's not just that the sentences are short and direct here as well. There are other stylistic choices in play. O'Brien avoids speaker tags (phrases such as "he said" and "she said") and so speeds up the conversation. He uses italics to emphasize certain words. The characters speak in fragments rather than always in complete sentences.

The benefits of close reading for style are numerous: it makes students better writers, it helps them understand what's going on in this story and in other stories, it allows them to perform well on analytical sections of the AP exam or other standardized tests, it gives them an appreciation for the craft of the writer. But above all, there is one goal in our minds when we engage students in exercises designed to examine style: we want them to *want* to read. The student who comes to an understanding and appreciation not just of what O'Brien writes about but also of *how* he writes about it is more likely to pick up the next book by this author or any other and keep reading—that's the prize for taking the time to examine language closely.

Within the Novel: Narrative Structure

For students, encountering new ways to structure storytelling can be both rewarding and intimidating. We tend to train students to think of storytelling linearly—stories have beginnings, middles, and ends, and are generally told in that order, beginning with "Once upon a time" and ending with "happily ever after." Even though television shows, movies, and books increasingly vary this structure, and even though authors since Virgil have been playing with the chronology of the stories they tell, it helps to discuss with students how and why authors vary structure. With a book like *The Things They Carried*, a discussion of structure is vital.

Clearly, the events of O'Brien's novel do not occur in a strictly linear fashion. What makes *The Things They Carried* more complicated than usual, however, is that the chronology of events is not the only way in which the author challenges our expectations. There is, despite what some students may believe on their first reading, a loose chronology to the events in the novel that occur in Vietnam, but O'Brien also keeps the reader slightly off balance by shifting point of view, voice, the length of chapters, even setting.

The approach described below works well once students have read the entire novel. You could also adapt the method to create a running story map as students read each story, though we like to wait to discuss structure so as not to sap the novel's overall strength for first-time readers. Once students have finished the work, however, we begin a discussion of the novel with this sort of overview:

1. Divide the class into four groups (or more—you can always have two groups work on the same activity and then compare results).

2. Assign each group an aspect of structure:

   ▪ Group 1: Chronology

   ▪ Group 2: Point of View

   ▪ Group 3: Length

   ▪ Group 4: Metafiction

3. Have each group categorize the twenty-two chapters of *The Things They Carried*. (Note: Because group 1 faces a more difficult task than the others, you could subdivide the chronology assignment and have two groups handle eleven chapters each.) Group 1 should identify, for each chapter, when the story is set—before, during, or after the war, or even the month or year if possible. This group should also identify any flashbacks

that take place within the chapters; some chapters begin after the war but flash back to an event from the war itself. Group 2 should list the stories told in first person and those told in third. Group 3 should group the stories by length (for instance, short chapters of less than five pages, medium-length chapters of between five and fifteen pages, long chapters of more than fifteen pages). Group 4 should identify those stories that contain elements of—or are entirely composed of—metafiction.

Group 1's product, for instance, might look something like this:

Stories that take place during a designated time in the war: "The Things They Carried" (April), "Enemies" (July), "Friends" (October), "The Dentist" (February), "Stockings" (October), "The Ghost Soldiers" (November–March), "Night Life" (sometime after March)

Stories that take place during the war but without a particular chronological setting: "Spin," "How to Tell a True War Story," "Sweetheart of the Song Tra Bong," "Church," "The Man I Killed," "Style," "In the Field" (Note: "Sweetheart" takes place before O'Brien joins Alpha company, but the other stories seem to occur more or less in chronological order as they appear. "Spin" and "How to Tell a True War Story" include moments from the narrator's life after the war.)

Stories that take place before the war: "On the Rainy River," "The Lives of the Dead"

Stories that take place after the war: "Love," "Ambush" (includes a flashback to the war), "Speaking of Courage," "Notes," "Good Form," "Field Trip"

4. On the board, make a chart with four columns, one for each group, and have the students fill in information for each story. Students can copy the chart on notebook paper. For your reference, here's how such a chart might look:

Chapter Title	Time	Point of View	Length	Metafiction?
"The Things They Carried"	During the war	3rd	long (26)	No
"Love"	After the war	1st	short (4)	No
"Spin"	Mostly during the war, references to present	1st/3rd	medium (7)	Yes
"On the Rainy River"	Before the war	1st	long (22)	No
"Enemies"	During the war (*July*)	3rd	short (3)	No
"Friends"	During the war (*October*)	3rd	short (2)	No
"How to Tell a True War Story"	Mostly during the war, references to present	1st	long (19)	Yes
"The Dentist"	During the war (*February*)	1st	short (3)	No
"Sweetheart of the Song Tra Bong"	During the war (*but before other war stories*)	3rd	long (27)	No (though the characters discuss storytelling)

"Stockings"	During the war (*end of October*)	1st	short (2)	No
"Church"	During the war	1st	short (5)	No
"The Man I Killed"	During the war	1st	medium (8)	No
"Ambush"	After the war (*with flashback*)	1st	short (4)	Yes
"Style"	During the war	1st	short (2)	No
"Speaking of Courage"	After the war	3rd	long (17)	No
"Notes"	After the war	1st	medium (7)	Yes
"In the Field"	During the war	3rd	long (17)	No
"Good Form"	After the war	1st	short (2)	Yes
"Field Trip"	After the war	1st	medium (8)	No
"The Ghost Soldiers"	During the war (*November–March*)	1st	long (29)	No
"Night Life"	During the war (*after March*)	3rd	medium (6)	No
"The Lives of the Dead"	Before the war	1st	long (21)	Yes

5. Once the entire chart is finished, ask students to consider this as a map of the novel. Discuss some of the questions raised by such a map:

   ▨ Do you see patterns, repetition, or signs of deliberate planning by the author? If so, what are they? Can you theorize about the effects O'Brien is trying to achieve through the placement of the stories or the way he tells them?

   ▨ How do the stories told in third person differ from those told in first person? Why might O'Brien choose to remove himself as a character from some stories but not others?

- Look at those stories that clearly appear outside of the general, overall chronology established in the novel. Why might O'Brien place these stories where he does? Why, in particular, is the last story a tale from the narrator's childhood?

- Is there an overall thematic thread that develops throughout the novel? How are the themes reinforced by structural decisions?

The point of such an exercise is not to be reductive; one can't replace the sensations of chaos in war by viewing the chaos logically. Rather, the idea is to give students a framework for and comfort zone with what may be a new model of storytelling. The framework may also provide an opening to discuss other unique ways of approaching storytelling; students might consider the effects of the frame narrative structure in *Heart of Darkness* or *Frankenstein*, the multiple narrators of *The Joy Luck Club* or *As I Lay Dying*, the use of flashback in *Death of a Salesman*, or the shifts in focus and scale in *The Grapes of Wrath*.

The Things They Carried does not represent O'Brien's only experiment with structure and storytelling. In *The Nuclear Age*, he creates a series of structured flashbacks, each getting closer to the present; in other novels, such as *In the Lake of the Woods*, *Tomcat in Love*, or *July, July*, he carefully places flashbacks to the war as key pieces of a story set long afterward. While many of his novels include first-person narration, not all do; in *Tomcat in Love*, the first-person narration is integral to our understanding of the character, while third-person narration in *In the Lake of the Woods* serves to heighten the sense of mystery.

Language, Violence, and Possible Challenges to Teaching O'Brien

In "How to Tell a True War Story," O'Brien defends his own use of coarse language:

> You can tell a true war story if it embarrasses you. If you don't care for obscenity, you don't care for the truth; if you don't care for the truth, watch how you vote. Send guys to war, they come home talking dirty. (69)

We're not suggesting that one can use this paragraph to allay the concerns of parents who object to profanity in their children's reading assignments, but the passage might make an interesting discussion point with the students themselves. Is it necessary for O'Brien to use obscenities? Violence? Is it appropriate?

The discussion concerning obscenity and O'Brien is one you've probably already had with your students, their parents, fellow teachers, and/or administrators involving other books. It is an inevitable experience when teaching teenagers who are coming in contact daily with issues that challenge them, their parents, and you. We often have to deal with this issue when teaching works by Mark Twain or William Faulkner, for instance. In an effort to have their stories and novels be of specific times and places, these writers created characters who speak as if they were real people, with curse words and racial slurs coming out of their mouths. The discussions you have with your students about offensive language are a necessary part of their education and one that should lead to a valuable lesson: how to interact with mature material in an adult manner.

In another book in this series, *Sandra Cisneros in the Classroom*, teacher and author Carol Jago puts it well: "The problem is that even when you win a censorship battle, you lose" (83). We teach *The Things They Carried* in classes for juniors and seniors in high school; we wouldn't recommend it for ninth graders. Even so, it's wise to take some precautions before introducing a book with graphic content:

- Make sure you've read the entire book and are familiar with any material that might cause difficulty for your students or their parents.

- Get the parents on your side. Consider writing a letter home explaining clearly why you think the work is worth studying and how it fits into the curriculum. Consider getting permission from parents for students to read the work (and consider alternate assignments for those whose parents object).

- Get administrators on your side. Present your case to your principal or department chair before beginning your study. The support of an entire English department for teaching a work can be a powerful statement.

- Get the students on your side. Discuss the challenges with them head-on. Ask questions about why certain scenes or words are integral to the story. You don't have to use the language in question to discuss its purpose.

- Check to see whether the National Council of Teachers of English (www.ncte.org) and its constituent committee, SLATE, have created any documents or other support materials for the work. If they haven't, you can contact NCTE for help should a challenge arise.

- Also consider possible challenges to any ancillary materials you use in class: websites, other readings about Vietnam, or movies.

Writing about Style

A final thought: consider assigning students the task of writing essays about style. Most teachers, we've found, shy away from this type of analysis. Essay topics tend to be about characterization, the ambiguities of theme, or how a plot develops. Essays probably should relate to overall meaning and theme in some way, but there are other possibilities. Here are some we've used:

- Assign a particular rhetorical device or strategy to each student. Have the students find numerous uses of those devices—metaphor, for instance, or repetition or closed syntax—and discuss in an essay how that device or strategy relates to the overall ideas in the work.

- Assign one story and ask students to discuss the overall meaning of the story through a discussion of three (or more) aspects of style.

- Write a comparison between two noticeably different chapters or between one of the stories in *The Things They Carried* and another, related work—a Hemingway short story, for instance. Require that at least one point of comparison (or maybe all points, leading to a conclusion that discusses theme and meaning) focus on stylistic elements and choices.

One effective way to promote an awareness of literary style is through a *dialectic journal*. Often used by AP teachers, this journal requires students to write down samples of the text they're reading using two or more columns. For instance, a student might write down a line he or she finds interesting in the first column. Then, at that point or later, the student can add a reflection on why the line is important—what it achieves—in the second column. Even later, the student could find the technical name for the device used in the line and add it to the third column. There are numerous variations to this journaling method, but all encourage students to think not just about *what* is interesting or unique in a work but also about *how* and *why* language creates meaning. An emphasis on style takes time, more time than simply discussing the overall theme of a work, but ultimately it can result in one of the richest rewards for any student approaching an author or text for the first time.

5 Taking a Critical Stance

> *"People don't talk in terms of critical responses; they just laugh, or they don't. . . . Essentially, you want books to generate not just intellectual but visceral or emotional responses."* (Lindbloom)

The opening quotation, from an interview conducted shortly after the publication of Tim O'Brien's novel *Tomcat in Love*, makes an interesting discussion starter or writing prompt for a class studying one of the author's books. Is O'Brien correct about the way "people" (or, in our case, students) talk? On the one hand, of course, we want students to have exactly the "emotional" response to literature the novelist describes—otherwise, why read at all? On the other hand, one of the great challenges every teacher faces is engaging students in intellectual discourse, especially written discourse, and convincing those same students to *care* about such a conversation. It's worth pointing out that O'Brien doesn't exclude the intellectual response, even if he seems to value, in this case, the "visceral or emotional" attitudes of readers as much or more.

And, after all, what writer will praise every response to his work without qualification, unless all of the reviews are positive?

Teachers ask students to write essays all the time. The point of such writing exercises probably seems fairly obvious to educators; an essay on a work of literature is at once a tool for assessment, reflection, conversation, and critical analysis—or so we hope. We should wonder, however, if such rationales for writing assignments are as obvious to students. If the conversation takes place only between the student and teacher, if the teacher (as sole audience) responds by marking mainly technical aspects of the analysis (or if the student chooses to see only such marks, and not more general comments), if the analysis is weak because the student sees the task as following a formula and not engaging in an intellectual exercise, then the essay as an assignment becomes no more than that—an assignment, to be hurried through and turned in with fingers crossed.

The three sections of this chapter address means of getting students to become part of a larger conversation, an ongoing discussion between critics, reviewers and readers. By examining the value of secondary sources, responding to those sources, and then writing in reaction and emulation, students not only enter the conversation but also may learn to value the process of writing for its purpose and potential audience.

Evaluating Sources

Part of the value of teaching a contemporary novel is the variety of immediate and important responses that is readily available. Does *The Things They Carried* belong in the canon of literature alongside *Moby-Dick* and *The Adventures of Huckleberry Finn* (two novels O'Brien himself often mentions in interviews)? The answer needn't be yes simply because the book has been assigned by a teacher; students can easily be directed to resources that will help them decide for themselves. In the case of O'Brien, a simple trip to the writer's homepage (http://www.illyria.com/tobhp.html) results in immediate access to the following:

- Reviews of the novels from major publications such as *Time* magazine and the *New York Times*

- Critical analysis of the historical and literary aspects of the novels

- Interviews with the author

- Speeches and articles by the author

- Teaching ideas and study guides

- Biographical resources

In fact, if anything, the sheer number of resources can be a bit daunting. What teachers can do to make the material manageable is help direct students in their research, interpretation, and discussion of such resources. The payoff is worthwhile—besides a deeper understanding of and connection to a novel, students may gain the sense of a true intellectual give-and-take. Essays and similar assignments such as book reviews (written in imitation of actual critical reviews) can become more than just an assignment; they can become part of an ongoing discussion, a discussion in which the student has a unique and important voice.

In reading such critical material, it's important to help students ask critical questions:

- What can you find out about the author of the critical work and the original publication site of the material? How "legitimate" is the source? Does the author bring any apparent biases to the response?

- Who is the intended audience for the material? How might that affect the way the author presents his or her ideas?

- When was the source published? Is the information current or out of date?

■ Are the ideas and arguments valid, objective, and impartial? If the content includes opinions, are they well reasoned and presented as such? What kinds of reasoning are employed?

■ To what extent does the author support his or her ideas with evidence? Does the author provide footnotes and/or a bibliography?

■ Is the source well written and error-free?

By answering these questions, students move from searching mainly for the information in sources to analyzing the sources themselves; in this way, they move a step closer to engaging in a dialogue with other legitimate voices rather than simply reporting what has already been said.

Take, as an example, the following excerpt from the original *New York Times* review of O'Brien's first book, *If I Die in a Combat Zone*:

> O'Brien brilliantly and quietly evokes the footsoldier's daily life in the paddies and foxholes, evokes a blind, blundering war: a Vietcong girl tries to squeeze the blood out to hurry her death, while the man who shot her strokes her hair; a friendly village is mistakenly shelled by its American protectors, killing many children. In the midst of this O'Brien can still find a kind of heroism in a quiet infantry captain, and some reassurance in the discovery that, like many soldiers, he could sometimes be brave.
>
> ---
>
> Source: Annie Gottlieb. "Two Sides of a Modern Disaster." *New York Times on the Web* 1 July 1973. 18 Feb. 2006 <http://www.nytimes.com/books/98/09/20/specials/obrien-combat.html>.

The author of this passage makes several assertions: O'Brien evokes images of the war "brilliantly," he evokes them "quietly," he finds "a kind of heroism" and "some reassurance." One might begin by asking students to identify these assertions, and then follow up with questions like these:

- To what extent does the author support these assertions? What proof is offered that O'Brien writes "brilliantly" or "quietly"?

- How informed are we by this passage? What do we know about the book that we did not know before? What useful or critical information that we might want do we *not* receive from this passage?

- What is the purpose of this paragraph; is it to make us want to read the book, to argue a thematic point, or both? How successful is it in its purpose?

Now compare the passage above to the following excerpt from Grace Paley's review of *The Nuclear Age* in the same publication:

What's wrong here? Is it my sense of the history of that period, my own experience of the deep-in and far-out women and men I knew and still know? It seems as though Mr. O'Brien has become afraid of the political meaning of William's sensible madness. Where William is consistently clear-sighted (which means he is more and more not out of his mind but out of the world's mind), Mr. O'Brien becomes devious and settles for mockery which usually means easy narrow characterization. In the case of the women this was particularly painful to me. William's love of Bobbi, the blonde poetry-writing stewardess, and his long pursuit of her seem fictionally just right. But the other women, his political comrades, are overly unattractive or extraordinarily beautiful. They seem to be the interfering author's clichéd decision. This is a tack a writer would take who is not particularly interested in the life and art of the nuclear age—or in any age for that matter. I believe that Mr. O'Brien is profoundly interested and probably dark with grief because of it, so I'm sorry to see these easy flaws.

Source: Grace Paley. "Digging a Shelter and a Grave." *New York Times on the Web* 17 Nov. 1985. 3 Oct. 2005 <http://www.nytimes.com/books/98/09/20/specials/obrien-nuclear.html>.

A similar set of questions might be asked by way of comparison:

- What assertions about the work does Paley make? Does she support those assertions? Does the review inform us as well as we'd wish? Are we convinced, for instance, by the assertions that O'Brien becomes "devious" or relies on clichés?

- How does this excerpt compare to the first passage? Is it more successful or less in achieving its purpose? Why?

In the case of both passages, the purpose of the review is to express an opinion, to pass judgment. That's a different goal from a scholarly article or book that may presuppose the quality of writing in the novel and seek to clarify a thematic argument; it's different, too, from the comments of an interviewer seeking to draw out information about a novel or the writing process. Students need to consider those distinctions and then make further distinctions; within the confines of the piece's purpose, is it successful? Is it a legitimate source?

It's easy, by the way, to find reviews and articles that praise Tim O'Brien's work, especially in response to *The Things They Carried*—easier in many ways than finding writers who are disparaging of his writing. But how many times can an author be called "brilliant" before the label begins to wear thin? In selecting sources for students to review or in guiding students' selections, you might want to seek out legitimate sources that raise questions about the work as well as answering them.

No matter which of the preceding reviews you prefer, if either, the student response to such writing is likely to be different from the response to a journal article or scholarly book. Reviews rely on a personal voice and individual assessment. A student reaction should probably include the same, though students might learn that a review also requires substantiation, logical reasoning, and a compelling argument. See the writing ideas at the end of this chapter for more ways of using the review process with students, as well as ideas for formal writing assignments such as those offered in response to the excerpts from academic writing below.

Responding to Critical Analysis

The hundreds of pages of interviews and reviews one finds through a quick Internet search are a fine place to start a study of O'Brien, but a bit of deeper research reveals scholarly and more in-depth scrutiny of the writer's work in numerous journal articles and books. High school students ready to grapple with O'Brien's sophisticated language and themes may also be ready to grapple with this level of critical analysis and the nuanced argumentation it can entail.

The following excerpts come from a variety of print sources; mostly, they are written in reaction to *The Things They Carried*, though the authors are certainly aware of O'Brien's other works. We've purposefully chosen passages from sources that raise questions of meaning, interpretation, and response.

Take, for instance, Lorrie N. Smith's comments on the response of female readers to *The Things They Carried*:

Reading 1: Gender

O'Brien—and his reviewers—seem curiously unselfconscious about this book's obsession with and ambivalence about representations of masculinity and femininity, particularly in the five stories originally published during the 1980s in *Esquire*. If this observation is accurate, and if, as one reviewer (Harris) claims, O'Brien's book "exposes the nature of all war stories," then we might postulate that "all war stories" are constituted by what Eve Kosofsky Sedgwick calls, in another context, a "drama of gender difference" (6). The book diverts attention from this central play by constructing an elaborate and captivating metafictional surface, but the drama is finally exposed by the sheer exaggeration and aggressiveness of its gendered roles and gendering gestures. "The things" his male characters "carried" to war, it turns out, include plenty of patriarchal baggage. O'Brien purports to tell "true" war stories, but stops short of fully interrogating their ideological underpinnings—either in terms of the binary construction of gender that permeates representations of war in our culture, or in terms of the Vietnam War itself as a political event implicated in racist, ethnocentric assumptions. Hence, the text offers no challenge to a discourse of war in which apparently innocent American men are tragically wounded and women are objectified, excluded, and silenced. My intent in bringing this subtext to light is not to devalue O'Brien's technical skill or emotional depth, but to account for my own discomfort as a female reader and to position *The Things They Carried* within a larger cultural project to rewrite the Vietnam War from a masculinist and strictly American perspective.

. . . All readers are to some extent subjugated by O'Brien's shifty narrator: however, the female reader, in particular, is rendered marginal and mute, faced with the choice throughout the book of either staying outside the story or reading against herself from a masculine point of view. O'Brien repeatedly inscribes the outsider as female, hence reinforcing masculine bonds that lessen the survivor/outsider distinction for male readers. Male characters are granted many moments of mutual understanding, whereas women pointedly won't, don't, or can't understand war stories. In short, O'Brien writes women out of the war and the female reader out of the storytelling circle.

Source: Lorrie N. Smith. "The Things Men Do: The Gendered Subtext in Tim O'Brien's *Esquire* Stories." *Critique* 36 (1994): 16–17. Reprinted with permission of Heldref Publications.

How does Smith's purpose, audience, and argument differ from those of a *New York Times* book review? There's a different level of formality here, the kind we probably want students to emulate in their own formal essay writing. There's also an interesting take on the novels that might provoke thoughtful discussion, journaling, or personal essay writing. Following are two ways we have framed assignments in response to this excerpt that produced different types of writing from students.

Writing Prompt: Personal

■ While reading *The Things They Carried*, did you have a sense of being included or excluded because of your gender? Do you think readers who do feel excluded are legitimate in criticizing the author's attitudes, real or implied, toward females? Explain your answer.

Writing Prompt: Formal

■ Are female readers of O'Brien's work in fact "rendered marginal or mute," as Smith claims? Drawing on specific female characters and scenes from the novel, discuss what role—if any—gender plays in the overall meaning of *The Things They Carried* and in the responses of its audience.

The following excerpts also come from scholarly journals or books that focus on *The Things They Carried*. The writing prompts that follow each passage elicit both personal and formal responses. A note about these prompts: Some may seem to ask for one-word answers ("Is it true that . . . ?"). Posing questions for an oral discussion in this way might not foster discussion without further prompting from the teacher. In writing, however, we constantly ask students to take stances on issues and to defend their answers—many external testing sources, such as the writing portion of AP, SAT, and state-required examinations, expect students to defend a stance in the same way. Considering the answer prompted by a question and the answer *expected* by the questioner is a valuable step for both teachers and student writers.

Reading 2: Historical Amnesia

To R. Z. Sheppard in *Time*, O'Brien succeeds "in conveying the free-fall sensation of fear and the surrealism of combat."

And Julian Loose in the *Times Literary Supplement* explains that "By creating a work which so adroitly resists finality, O'Brien has been faithful to Vietnam and the stories told about it." For these reviewers, the war is a messy, unreal conflict that resists finality.

To describe the mass bombardment, defoliation, systematic assassinations, and planned destruction of the rural society of South Vietnam as "messy," however, is to domesticate it, to make it seem the result of bad management. It also views the war from an American perspective and profoundly trivializes the suffering of the Vietnamese. Nonetheless, this perception is an accurate assessment from the point of view of imperialists, for whom Vietnam was a "messy" war (as opposed to the "splendid, little war" the United States fought against Spain at the turn of the century or the alleged surgical precision of the Persian Gulf War) because it did not go as planned and, for a brief time, became something of an obstacle for American policy makers, a mess they have been trying to wash their hands of ever since.

Source: Jim Neilson. *Warring Fictions: American Literary Culture and the Vietnam War Narrative.* Jackson: University Press of Mississippi, 1998. 195–96.

Writing Prompts

■ To what extent does O'Brien, through inclusion or exclusion of details about the Vietnamese during the war, trivialize "the suffering of the Vietnamese" and create an ethnocentric work? Do you think the novelist bears a responsibility for presenting multiple points of view equally?

▦ Is the Vietnam War, as presented in this novel, "a messy, unreal conflict that resists finality"? Discuss the accuracy of this characterization of *The Things They Carried* using examples such as narrative structure and the attitudes of the characters.

Reading 3: Issues of Morality

Notwithstanding the apparent insignificance Tim O'Brien attaches to such tales, and despite a comment in his latest novel, *The Things They Carried*, that "a true war story is never moral" (1990, 76), the best war stories, fiction and nonfiction, contain important lessons about war—if readers pay attention. More important, as Herr notes, these stories tell readers a lot about people, including the storytellers. The best tales, whether told by participants and observers remembering war or by artists imagining the experiences, cut through ideological cant and battlefield action to explore the often disturbing, ambiguous, and complex elements of war, human behavior, and life. They tell of courage, fear, cowardice, self-sacrifice, evil, life, death, and war's obscenity, as well as its attraction. A few of these stories contain occasional humorous anecdotes about war. Others are confessionals, as storytellers pour out their exhilaration, physical pain, emotional suffering, or guilt related to the experience. Most reduce war to basic issues: participants instinctively struggling to kill and survive and in the process sinking to ignominious depths of evil; rising to glorious moments of self-sacrifice, compassion, and honor; or routinely existing on the battlefield. The result is a fundamental sympathy for combat soldiers as fallible human beings living within the crucible of war.

Source: Tobey C. Herzog. *Vietnam War Stories: Innocence Lost*. London: Routledge, 1992. 2.

Writing Prompts

- Are there ultimately morals in the stories and novels of Tim O'Brien? Specifically, what morals or lessons do you take away from your reading of his works?

- To what extent does *The Things They Carried* "reduce war to basic issues" of death, survival, courage, and honor? Using textual evidence, refute, support, or qualify the idea that the novel ultimately aims to present such basic concepts.

Reading 4: Genre

O'Brien is not at all sure of the strength of the walls erected by clear-cut genre distinctions. A number of the separately published chapters of *Carried* dissolve the wall separating essay and fiction. We often find ourselves in what O'Brien calls the "no-man's land between" the two, "between Cleveland Heights and deep jungle." We "come up on the edge of something" and "swirl back and forth across the border" (115). . . . It is precisely because of his liminal uncertainty that the author could not make *Carried* memoir or fiction, essay or story, autobiography or metafiction, no more than he knew while on the Rainy River if he was in the United

States or Canada. The line separating genres is at most a dotted, wavering one.

Source: Don Ringnalda. *Fighting and Writing the Vietnam War*. Jackson: University Press of Mississippi, 1994. 93.

Writing Prompts

■ To what extent do the confines of genre determine how we read a text? What preconceptions did you have before reading *The Things They Carried*, what did you expect of the work after reading only the first chapter, and how were those expectations supported or challenged by the time you finished reading?

■ How would you define *The Things They Carried*: as a collection of stories, as a novel, as a mixture of fiction and nonfiction, or in some other way? What evidence from the text can you offer to support an argument about how the structure of the work should be viewed?

Reading 5: Language and Storytelling

In the end O'Brien doesn't trust language. In 1994, during his return trip to Vietnam, O'Brien stands in front of a ditch at My Lai, "where maybe 50, maybe 80, maybe 100 innocent human beings perished." He focusses on the facts: 504 dead—"women, infants, teenagers, old men"—in an area that saw civilian casualties "approaching 50,000 a year" (52). Words fail him. Words can't express the misery, words can't make a difference: "I want a miracle. That's the final emotion. The terror at this ditch, the certain doom, the need for God's intervention," and the unstated fear that it will never come ("Vietnam" 53). O'Brien's response, the response of the woman with him, the response of the Vietnamese survivors with him, is silence. Language can do nothing. It cannot adequately express, it cannot change the facts, it cannot redeem anything. There is no saving of these dead souls, or of anyone's living soul. As crucial and powerful as imagination and language are, O'Brien's writing, in the end, reveals their limitations.

Source: Alex Vernon. "Salvation, Storytelling, and Pilgrimage in Tim O'Brien's *The Things They Carried*." *Mosaic* 36 (2003): 185.

Writing Prompts

- Do you agree that imagination and language are limited? Do you agree that O'Brien suggests they are?

- To what extent, if any, does language offer redemption for the narrator or characters in *The Things They Carried*?

Further Writing: Reviews and Essays
Reviews

As opinion pieces, reviews lend themselves to discussion and conversation in the classroom. Most actual book reviews, such as those included in this chapter, contain some plot summary and basic description; many also include a few salient biographical facts about the author. Such information is not out of place in student-written reviews, but it must not eclipse the more important elements of the review—the reviewer's assessment of the material and supporting evidence.

We use the following assignments as a means of introducing students to the review process:

- With a partner, find a review of the work from a legitimate source such as a major newspaper or magazine. Identify and discuss with your partner the main assertion of the review. Then, using textual evidence to support your opinion, write a response in which you disagree with the opinion of the reviewer while your partner writes a response agreeing with the opinion (or vice versa—you may agree while your partner disagrees).

- Choose a single story (or chapter) from *The Things They Carried*. Write your own review of the story in which you briefly summarize or describe the plot, setting, and characters, and then state your opinion of the quality of the overall piece, including relevant questions, criticisms, or praise. Support your opinion with details from the story.

You might also consider adopting one of the following strategies for provoking class discussion of reviews:

- Choose an interesting or controversial review of the novel. As a class, number the assertions or opinions offered by the reviewer— ideally, you'll be able to find at least five to ten separate statements. Then have each student count the number of statements or assertions with which he or she agrees. Line students up in order: those who agree with none of the statements at one end of the line, those who agree with one next, those who agree with two next, and so on. Then discuss each statement or assertion individually—the line will allow you to balance the discussion between those who mostly agree with the reviewer and those who mostly disagree; it will also encourage more students to speak out, since their opinions are already somewhat visible. At the end of the discussion, ask what the overall shape of the line (is it balanced or weighted to one side or another) suggests about the overall quality of the reviewer's opinions and writing.

- Have different groups read and discuss different, possibly contradictory, reviews of a work. Then discuss the overall quality of the work as a class, asking students to use the reviews as support. As the discussion progresses, ask students to consider how the opinions of others shape our own responses to the works we read and suggest ways of becoming critical consumers of reviews and information about the works they read.

On-Demand Essays

As timed writing assessments in response to open-ended prompts, such as those on the AP exams or SAT, become more common, it's a good idea even for pre-AP teachers to use such prompts as practice. Though students taking the AP English Literature test, for instance, can choose any novel or play of literary merit as a focus for the forty-minute essay, the format works with classes studying individual works of literature as well. Here are some samples of this type of prompt, each of which could be applied to *The Things They Carried* as well as other O'Brien works:

- In many works of literature, a physical journey serves not only to further the plot but also to reinforce themes or ideas in the story. Choose a work of literary merit in which travel from one place to another plays an important role and, in a well-organized essay, discuss how the physical movement of the characters reveals or heightens internal discoveries or investigation.

- The last chapter of Tim O'Brien's *The Things They Carried* begins, "But this too is true: stories can save us." Choose a novel or play of literary merit in which a character relies on storytelling to achieve salvation or redemption. In a well-organized essay, discuss the relationship between the act of storytelling and the character's moral development.

- Some novels or plays manipulate the structure through which a story is told by rearranging events, using multiple points of view, mixing genres, or otherwise departing from the structure expected by the reader. Choose a work of literary merit and discuss the narrative and structural techniques used by the author and how those techniques depart from convention in an attempt to convey the overall meaning of the work.

Formal and Personal Essay Topics

The following questions and essay topics might be phrased as prompts for either formal or personal essays:

- Many of the stories in *The Things They Carried* and other works by Tim O'Brien explore the concept of courage. What, for the author, ultimately constitutes courage?

- Of all the stories in *The Things They Carried*, which presents the greatest emotional challenge to the reader; in other words, which is most difficult to read? Why?

- The story "On the Rainy River" begins with a description of O'Brien's summer job in a pig slaughterhouse and ends with his decision to go to the war. How are these two aspects of the story connected?

- How does the final story, "The Lives of the Dead," relate thematically to the rest of *The Things They Carried*? Does this story qualify, according to O'Brien's description, as a "true war story"?

- Why do you think O'Brien dedicates *The Things They Carried* to the characters who appear in the book?

- In a 1994 article, O'Brien wrote about contemplating suicide. Based on your reading of his work, does this contemplation surprise you?

- Several deaths are mentioned numerous times in *The Things They Carried*—most notably the deaths of Kiowa and the Vietnamese soldier O'Brien claims to have killed. Why do you think the author dwells on these deaths in particular, and how do the multiple versions of the deaths reinforce the meaning of the work as a whole?

- Tim O'Brien has claimed to be a writer who writes about love, not war. Is this claim accurate?

6 The Author's Voice: Interviews and Recollections

■ ■

Imagine the different form your approach to teaching, say, *The Canterbury Tales* might take if Geoffrey Chaucer regularly sat down to answer the questions of reporters, students, and readers and the transcripts were printed or posted online. On the one hand, some tricky passages or ideas might suddenly be illuminated, while on the other, new questions of interpretation or context could easily arise.

One of the wonderful aspects of teaching the works of a living author is not only that we have a chance to read his or her reflections on specific texts and the craft of writing, but also that the author's reflections and approach may change even as we're studying the work. Interviews with Tim O'Brien, as well as addresses and speeches by the author, are numerous, easy to find, and enriching for classroom discussions. We've chosen the following samples by topic; any one of them might make an interesting discussion or writing starter for a class studying the author's work.

At the end of this chapter, after the interview excerpts, you'll find some specific ideas for using interviews with students.

On Reading

QUESTION: Have you found yourself consciously influenced by your reading knowledge of war? Say Stephen Crane, Tolstoy, etc?

O'Brien: Not really. But when I read the best things by Crane or Tolstoy, I feel a sense of confirmation. That is, Vietnam happened to me twenty years ago, or more, and I wonder sometimes what did happen then. Was it real? Am I writing bullshit? Are my memories accurate? And when I read a good piece of literature, it reminds me of what I've been through and what civilizations, not just people, have gone through—that in fact all of us, in all our lives, whether we're personally serving in a war or not, have gone through the threat of war, the threat of annihilation, the threat of human violence. Good writing about the subject shows me that I'm not utterly mistaken, that I'm not wandering off alone, down this silly path. It tells me I'm not mistaken to pursue these emotions. But it's not war so much I'm thinking about here. It's violence, which is around all of us. It's in our genes, this sense that we're all going to die some day.

Source: "A Conversation with Tim O'Brien." Interview with Daniel Bourne and Debra Shostak. *Artful Dodge* 2 Oct. 1991. 15 Mar. 2006 <http://www.wooster.edu/artfuldodge/interviews/obrien.htm>.

On Writing

Question: Could you explain your writing process?

O'Brien: Well the process is really very simple. I get up in the morning and go to work around 7:30, I work until about two. I take a break, I work out, I work again until about six or so. I do that every day, all week, Saturday and Sunday, holidays, all the time. It's a full time job.

Source: "Ten Questions with Tim O'Brien." Interview with Patrick Hunt. *Flyer News* [U of Dayton student newspaper]. 10 Oct. 2003. 20 Apr. 2006 <http://www.flyernews.com/article.php?section=AE&volume=51&issue=9&artnum=01>.

QUESTION: I was going to ask what you thought about that old adage that a writer has to suffer, but what you've just said pretty much answers my question—that writing war stories isn't so much about theme but the fact that dramatically you're almost immediately on this terrain of life and death.

O'BRIEN: Yes, that's true, a writer does have to suffer. As we all do. We all stub our toes, we all have people who don't love us enough. There are all kinds of suffering; life is a bunch of suffering. There are a lot of other things too, of course, but we all suffer. And stories are ordinarily made out of suffering. I'm trying to think of one that isn't, and I can't. Bambi? Well, Bambi loses his mommy, right? Burned up in a forest fire? I think that's what happens. All the fairy tales we grow up with, these little things we think we treat our kids to are just filled with suffering. Goldilocks, lost in the woods. What could be more terrifying: a little girl lost in the woods with a bunch of bears? That's essentially what stories are about. That is not to say it's the suffering alone; but it's the premise of a certain way of storytelling, how we deal with conflict and with struggle and tensions in our lives.

Source: "A Conversation with Tim O'Brien." Interview with Daniel Bourne and Debra Shostak. *Artful Dodge* 2 Oct. 1991. 15 Mar. 2006 <http://www.wooster.edu/artfuldodge/interviews/obrien.htm>.

On Writing about Women

QUESTION: Have you found it difficult to write from a woman's perspective?

O'BRIEN: No, easy as heck. You don't have to commit murder to write about murder, and you don't have to be a woman to write about being a woman. Flaubert proved it. Same for women—you don't have to be a man to write about men. That's probably why I love writing novels, is I can enter into other skins and other ways of looking at the world. God knows I did in this book, *Tomcat*, and that's one of the joys of being a writer, is you can enter into the head, say, of a woman having an affair or this newlywed I talked about. It's what makes me do this as opposed to, you know, doing non-fiction.

Source: "Interview with Tim O'Brien—From Life to Fiction." Interview with Karen Rosica. *Lighthouse Writers Newsletter* 29 Oct. 1994. 15 Mar. 2006 <http://www.lighthousewriters.com/newslett/timobrie.htm>.

On the Vietnam Experience

QUESTION: You've said that you haven't had the type of readjustment problems many veterans have had.

O'BRIEN: That's true. I think the reason for it is that I've been able to write about what happened to me. I was blessed with the natural outlet of being able to write stories, books, and essays about those experiences. Other men who served in Vietnam didn't have that outlet at all. They ended up staying silent, as John Wade does—hiding a lot, as he does, and withdrawing from their loved ones. I was among the very fortunate few who did have writing as an outlet. I'm not sure psychologically what would have happened to me if I hadn't had it. Who knows? It's a hypothetical question, so I'll never know.

Source: "In the Name of Love: An Interview with Tim O'Brien." Interview with Scott Sawyer. *Mars Hill Review* 4 Winter/Spring 1996: 117–26.

On Teaching

QUESTION: Is Vietnam in your books taken too literally?

O'Brien: Depends on the reader. My books are taught in schools—high schools and colleges—there's a tendency to do what you just said, over politicize the books and use them almost as history lessons. It's a bit like using *The Sun Also Rises* as a history lesson about the Lost Generation. It would be true in a way but it would undermine the artistry of the book. It's about Jake and Bret and their need for love.

QUESTION: It's a story.

O'BRIEN: Yeah, it's a story. And it's set then and you can talk about it in those terms. That's only one way of talking about it; if I close my eyes I see Jake and Bret at the end of the book sitting in a cab. The Lost Generation is a backdrop for it and it's all related—but it's about Jake and Bret.

Source: "Tim O'Brien: Author of *July, July* Talks with Robert Birnbaum." Interview with Robert Birnbaum. *Identitytheory.com* 5 Nov. 2002. 12 May 2006 <http://www.identitytheory.com/people/birnbaum72.html>.

O'BRIEN: Teaching writing is more intuitive than teaching mathematics. I teach pretty much the way I write, which is by trial and error. . . . I show them how to have more than one ball up in the air, to complicate the story and make it more like the lives we all lead, which are not uni-dimensional.

Source: Julia Hanna. "The Things He Carries." *Kennedy School Bulletin* Spring 2003. 1 May 2006 <http://www.ksg.harvard.edu/ksgpress/bulletin/spring2003/features/things.html>.

On Truth and Lies

QUESTION: I've read several of your books, and [I'm] very curious about how much is real and how much isn't real . . .

O'BRIEN: Yeah. Well, I'll respond in two ways. One—excuse me, my cold is hitting me now—(*coughs*) Excuse me. Number one, uh, the literal truth is ultimately, to me, irrelevant. What matters to me is the heart-truth. I'm going to die, you're all going to die, the earth is going to flame out when the sun goes. We all know the facts. The truth—I mean, does it matter what the real Hamlet was like, or the real Ulysses—does it matter? Well, I don't think so. In the fundamental human way, the ways we think about in our dream-lives, and our moral lives, and our spiritual lives, what matters is what happens in our hearts. A good lie, if nobly told, for good reason, seems to me preferable to a very boring and pedestrian truth, which can lie, too. That's one way of answering.

I'll give you a more practical answer. The last piece I read for you, it is very—and it does approximate an event that happened in my life, and it's hard for me to read to you, at the same time it wasn't literally true in all its detail. It wasn't a hand grenade, it was a, was a rifle thing. We had circled the village one night—called it cordoning the village—and this stuff never worked in Vietnam—those vets who are here know what I'm talking about—these things never worked, but it did, once. We circled the village and we drove the enemy out in daylight, and three enemy soldiers came marching—the silhouettes like you're at a carnival shoot—and about eighteen of us or twenty of us were lined up along a paddy dike. We all opened up from, I don't know, eighteen yards or twenty yards away. We, really, we killed one of them; the others we couldn't find, which shows you what bad shots we were on top of everything else. Well, I will never know whether I killed anyone, that man in particular—how do I know? I hope I didn't. But I'll never know.

The thing is, you have to, though, when you return from a war, you have to assume responsibility. I was there, I took part in it, I did pull the trigger, and whether I literally killed a man or not is finally irrelevant to me. What matters is I was part of it all, the machine that did it, and do feel a sense of obligation, and through that story I can share some of my feelings, when I walked over [to] that corpse that day, and looked down at it, wondering, thinking, "Dear God, dear God, please don't let it have been my bullet, dear God, please." Um, that's the second answer.

Source: Tim O'Brien. "Writing Vietnam." President's Lecture. Brown University, Providence. 21 Apr. 1999.

Using Interviews in the Classroom

Throughout the novel *In the Lake of the Woods*, O'Brien includes snippets of interviews, interrogations, and quoted passages not unlike those above; some of the interviews are fictional, others gleaned from actual historical documents ranging from the testimonies given by soldiers involved in the My Lai massacre to materials from the Geneva Convention and General Custer. O'Brien understands the power of hearing individual voices directly.

Take, for instance, this section of Paul Meadlo's court-martial from 1969, which O'Brien quotes at the start of one of the chapters called "Evidence":

Q: What did you do?

A: I held my M-16 on them.

Q: Why?

A: Because they might attack.

Q: They were children and babies?

A: Yes.

Q: And they might attack? Children and babies?

A: They might've had a fully loaded hand grenade on them. The mothers might have throwed them at us. (136)

Fiction is important; so are authentic voices that explain and illuminate events, whether those events include an episode in Vietnam or the writing of a novel. In the case of Tim O'Brien, students are fortunate to have so many opportunities for exposure to the author's own reflection on his work.

We use excerpts from the interviews cited previously, as well as interviews students find on their own using the Internet or other resources. Here are some possible approaches:

- Assign topics, such as those in the chapter headings, to students or pairs of students. Have each individual or pair search for one interesting statement by the author relevant to the topic and then share that statement with the class. Students might also, in their presentation of the statement, discuss their own feelings about the topic. Do they agree or disagree with O'Brien? Are they surprised or unsurprised by his viewpoints?

- Find enough different interviews with O'Brien for each student (or pair) to be assigned one—there are plenty available. Have each student or pair read an interview and then summarize the author's viewpoint toward, say, writing or Vietnam in general. Then share the distillations either orally or by making a time line for the whole class to see: arrange the summaries in chronological order and discuss whether anything O'Brien says seems to reflect that period in his career or in history.

- Ask students to write down ten questions they would ask the author if given the chance. Then compare their questions to those asked by actual interviewers. Which are the same? Which are different? Why might some interviewers ask different questions than others? How do your students think O'Brien might feel about the different questions in various interviews?

- Read the interview excerpt labeled "On the Vietnam Experience" above, in which O'Brien talks about "writing as an outlet." Then have students read the article written by the author for the *New York Times* in 1994 called "The Vietnam in Me," in which O'Brien discusses contemplating suicide. Why might an interview and an article written by the author seem to disagree with each other, if indeed these passages do disagree?

- Have students find adults who were alive during the Vietnam War (or during another war, such as World War II, the Gulf War, Korea, or even the cold war) and conduct interviews of their own. Have students compose questions beforehand, and consider for yourself and with the class how the interviews will be conducted, recorded, shared, and debriefed.

- Have students create an "interview" by posing questions about a character from, say, *The Things They Carried* and answering those questions with direct quotations from that character taken from the novel. The result of this assignment must include actual passages from the text, and therefore the assignment serves as a nice warm-up for an essay assignment in which students need to use quoted evidence to support their points.

7 Extensions and Connections

> *"Books are a little bit like our dreams and memories. They continue to live in our heads long after they've passed away. Like dead puppies from our childhood, or a set of friends from Vietnam, they operate on the ghost principle." (O'Brien, "In the Name of Love")*

Teaching Other O'Brien Works

Each of Tim O'Brien's novels touches on Vietnam in some way, though in some works the war itself plays a more pivotal role than in others. The publication of *The Things They Carried* clearly marked a pivotal moment in the writer's career; since 1990, O'Brien's works have focused, by and large, on aftershocks of the war intertwined with separate issues of morality and choice. Perhaps a clearer way for teachers to picture the author's body of works is by two simple categories: novels set during the war and novels set afterward.

Works Set during Vietnam

O'Brien has published three works that take place in and revolve around (for the most part, at least) the Vietnam War. His first book, *If I Die in a Combat Zone*, recounts the author's own journey from receiving his draft notice to serving in the infantry. Though the book is based closely on real events, O'Brien is among the first to point out that even real events must be fictionalized to some extent to be turned into a book. The work makes interesting reading for students who wish to explore further the experiences described in *The Things They Carried* or as a more true-to-life document of the experiences of Tim O'Brien the soldier.

After *If I Die in a Combat Zone*, O'Brien turned to fiction. Among his early works was the National Book Award winner of 1979, *Going After Cacciato* (it beat out the bestseller *The World According to Garp*). Some critics described the novel as an experiment in "magical realism"—it describes a fictional journey taken by a group of American soldiers in Vietnam chasing an AWOL platoon member from Asia to Europe. After *The Things They Carried*, *Going After Cacciato* is probably the most easily teachable of O'Brien's fictional works for high school classes; the classic journey motif makes for a nice comparison to other works, from *The Adventures of Huckleberry Finn* to *Cold Mountain*.

A third work, *The Nuclear Age*, contains no scenes that take place in Vietnam itself but revolves nonetheless around the Vietnam War; a major plot element in the story involves a group of radical war protestors. This work, while not as successful in the commercial market as *Going After Cacciato*, provides a different perspective of Vietnam with no moral simplicities.

Works Set after Vietnam

Of O'Brien's four works set mainly after the war, *In the Lake of the Woods*, the author's follow-up to *The Things They Carried*, is the only text to have appeared as a suggested work on the AP Literature exam. The novel garnered a good bit of critical acclaim. Its fictional premise (the main character has just lost a presidential election) is woven together with the aftershocks of Vietnam. Since the Vietnam War continues to figure into presidential and other national campaigns—both in terms of its resonance in national culture and identity and in the particular choices made by public figures during the period—*In the Lake of the Woods* provides any number of jumping-off points for research, discussion, and writing not only about the war itself but also about politics in the decades since.

The other three novels set after the war may provide slightly less rich ground for the high school teacher even if they are captivating for many adult readers: *Northern Lights*, an early book that was long out of print, examines the tensions between two brothers, a vet and a protestor; *Tomcat in Love* takes as its study a philandering, egomaniacal college professor; the middle-aged characters in *July, July* convene at a high school reunion. Each of these works is worthy of study; the author's spare voice, interest in structural approaches to storytelling, and fascination with the resonating issues of the Vietnam War inform and enrich all of his works. Nonetheless, most high school teachers will probably find *The Things They Carried*, *Going After Cacciato*, and *In the Lake of the Woods* most suited to their curricula.

A final note: Any study of O'Brien's writing should include the author's *New York Times* essay "The Vietnam in Me," published in 1994 and available online at http://www.nytimes.com/books/98/09/20/specials/obrien-vietnam.html?_r=1&oref=slogin. In it, the writer reflects on his return to Vietnam years after the war and offers rich connections between the real history of Vietnam, O'Brien's fictional accounts, and the role and life of the artist.

Teaching Other Novels about War

So much has been written in the United States about wars that offering a comprehensive list of war novels is impossible, but a quick look at some of the most commonly taught works revolving around war reveals that valuable connections to O'Brien's works are available—consider, for instance, some possible essay topics that we have used:

Catch-22 and *The Things They Carried*
> Compare the shifts in structure, point of view, and time in these two works. How do O'Brien and Joseph Heller attempt to convey the experiences and lessons of war through non-traditional methods of storytelling?
>
> The phrases "dark humor" or "black humor" are often used to describe the effect of combining morbid details with farce to create a sense of comical absurdity. Identify several scenes in each novel that are presented with dark humor. How do these authors use this effect in these scenes and throughout their works to convey their overall attitudes toward war?

Cold Mountain and *Going After Cacciato*
> Each of these works was compared by reviewers to Homer's *Odyssey* because each revolves around a soldier's journey. How do O'Brien and Charles Frazier use the episodic nature of the journeys and their resolutions to convey a sense of the toll war takes on soldiers?
>
> Unlike Odysseus, who undertook a journey after he finished fighting in war, characters in both of these novels desert. How do the authors use characterization and plot to discuss the nature of desertion and moral difficulties involved in war?

A Farewell to Arms and *The Things They Carried*
> Ernest Hemingway was both criticized and praised for his spare, "hard-boiled" style. Among the elements of this style,

for instance, are direct syntax, terse exchanges of dialogue, and the factual observation of the narrator. To what extent does O'Brien adopt a similarly hard-boiled style, and why might this style be appropriate for the subject matter of these novels?

James Joyce said of Hemingway: "He has reduced the veil between literature and life, which is what every writer strives to do." In what ways do O'Brien and Hemingway use war to "reduce the veil between literature and life"? Are they equally successful in doing so?

All Quiet on the Western Front and *Going After Cacciato* or *The Things They Carried*

The narrator of *All Quiet on the Western Front* says, "We were eighteen and had begun to love life and the world; and we had to shoot it to pieces." What role does the age of the characters play in these novels? How are the specific experiences, vocabulary, and attitudes of soldiers defined by their ages, and how do their ages in turn define the nature of warfare?

What techniques do Erich Maria Remarque and O'Brien use to contrast the intensity of battle with the daily lives of soldiers in combat-ready situations?

Connections work, of course, with other commonly taught works as well: *The Killer Angels, The Thin Red Line, The Red Badge of Courage, Johnny Tremain.* Here are a few questions that might help start a discussion or writing assignment comparing any of these works or other war novels to O'Brien's works:

- What makes a novel more than just a war story? How and why do authors use background or characterization to make war stories matter to us for reasons other than the mere survival of the characters?

- Why do so many novelists avoid the larger political issues at stake in wars and focus on personal stories?

- What is the place of women in war stories?

- What is the importance of choosing a title for a war novel? How do the titles of war stories you've read convey important information about the meanings of the works?

- To what extent do these novels emphasize the effects of war on those who are not soldiers? What is the role of the civilian in warfare?

- How is the government portrayed in these war stories? What attitudes do the characters and the author demonstrate toward the government?

- What common themes of war, such as loss of innocence or the definition of courage, can you compare and contrast using these works?

Vietnam in Film

Numerous films have depicted the events of the Vietnam War, but a few offer obvious connections to O'Brien's writing. One must be cautious, of course, since such films inevitably contain graphic material and profanity; at the same time, visual imagery of the chaos and violence of war can make powerful connections to written descriptions of battle and its effects on soldiers.

Consider showing excerpts of the following movies rather than the entire films in order to maximize thematic connections and allow time for debriefing:

Apocalypse Now

Besides the general sense of the absurdity and chaos of war that both this movie and several of O'Brien's works share, there are clear links in imagery and idea between the film and *The Things They Carried*: the slaughter of a water buffalo that mirrors an episode in "How to Tell a True War Story," the descent into the dark arena of human brutality and savagery in the story "Sweetheart of the Song Tra Bong" (see the section on linking to Conrad's *Heart of Darkness* below), and the repetition of the phrase "the horror," a word O'Brien also uses to define a "true" war story.

Platoon

As one of the first movies to focus exclusively on the experience of the common foot soldier in Vietnam, *Platoon* attempts to portray the realities of battle and also explores issues of moral decision making in the war. The shifting terrain of morality in warfare is common ground in O'Brien's stories as well.

Good Morning, Vietnam

There are combat scenes at the end of this movie, as well as harsh criticism of military bureaucracy, but the questions raised about the dark humor of soldiers in war may make for the best connection to O'Brien's work.

Teachers also sometimes use *Full Metal Jacket, Hamburger Hill, The Deer Hunter*, even excerpts from *Forrest Gump* (or, ranging further afield, *MASH*). Of course, veterans of the war are divided on the accuracy of all of these movies (and, after all, when was the last time you saw a movie about teaching that was entirely true to life?), but that also creates an opportunity for discussion: ask students to think or to ask someone involved in the war about the accuracies, inaccuracies, and biases of such movies.

In addition, with any film, you might consider debriefing with questions such as these:

- What aspects of warfare can be conveyed more effectively using visual imagery than writing, if any? Are there aspects of war that are better conveyed through the written word? Why?

- What themes seem to be common to Vietnam films and stories? How do movies use visual imagery, structural techniques, and tools such as sound tracks to enhance the exploration of these themes?

- How do movies or stories about Vietnam differ from movies or stories about other wars? Are there issues at stake in Vietnam stories that are not usually the focus of other stories?

- To what extent are the moral decisions of soldiers reinforced by the visual techniques of film?

- How do films use the point of view of the camera and characters to convey the experiences of war?

- How are the Vietnamese portrayed in films about the war? How does this compare to the portrayal of the Vietnamese in O'Brien's works? Are Americans vilified, celebrated, or treated as neutral?

- To what extent are protagonists of these movies heroic? How is the nature of heroism portrayed through story, dialogue, or the visual?

- To what extent can any movie re-create the actual experience of being in a war? Can movies do this more or less effectively than fictional or nonfictional accounts?

▨ Is the primary goal of a movie about Vietnam to capture the essence of the experience or to create a metaphor or lesson using the war as a backdrop? What *should* the goal of a war story be?

Thematic Links to the Canon

As *The Things They Carried* and other O'Brien works take their place amidst the commonly taught body of high school literature, teachers will naturally search for ways to connect works thematically, stylistically, and structurally. Here are some we've found:

Heart of Darkness

The link between Joseph Conrad's novel and O'Brien's can be firmly established through the viewing of *Apocalypse Now*, but even without the film as a bridge the connections are clear. Both are studies of the savagery and brutality that journeys away from civilization and into a stress-ridden wilderness can produce. O'Brien's chapter titled "Sweetheart of the Song Tra Bong" is almost a retelling of Marlow's journey; in this case, a cheerleader becomes a Kurtz-like figure.

Hamlet

There are battle scenes aplenty in Shakespeare, of course, but as with O'Brien, it's the moments of moral crisis that are captivating. Hamlet's contemplations of death, his hesitancy to kill, his dark humor in the face of unacceptable circumstances—all make for interesting connections between the young prince and young soldiers. The notions of courage raised by O'Brien are likewise comparable to themes in *Hamlet*.

The Storytelling Connection

O'Brien is not the first author to suggest that "stories can save us"—from *The Arabian Nights* to Isabel Allende, writers have been exploring the role of storytelling and the ways in which storytellers reveal themselves through the stories they tell. Consider having students make comparisons to the following works and the ways in which they present the art of storytelling: *Beowulf*, *The Canterbury Tales* (Chaucer), *Eva Luna* (Allende), *Life of Pi* (Yann Martel), *The Prince of Tides* (Pat Conroy), *The Blind Assassin* (Margaret Atwood).

Metafiction

We often pair chapters of *The Things They Carried* with other short stories that employ metafiction:

- "Elbow Room" by James Alan McPherson

- "How to Become a Writer" by Lorrie Moore

- "People Like That Are the Only People Here" by Lorrie Moore

- "How to Tell a Story" by Mark Twain

- "Laughing Man" by J. D. Salinger

- "The Fall of the House of Usher" by Edgar Allan Poe

Each of these stories contains heavy doses of metafiction, but they are quite different from one another. The pairing of such stories not only allows for interesting comparison and contrast writing assignments, but can also serve as a springboard for encouraging students to write their own metafictional reflections on work they've composed.

The Blurred Line between Fact and Fiction

Some teachers seem concerned that students will confuse what they read in fictional stories with actual historical events, and that may happen; however, many students enjoy stories precisely for the blurred lines, the tension between what is true and how it is portrayed, and eagerly enter discussions about such facets of contemporary writing. Among those novels which skirt the line between imagination and documented truth: *In Cold Blood* (Truman Capote), *A Heartbreaking Work of Staggering Genius* (Dave Eggers), *Bel Canto* (Ann Patchett), *All the King's Men* (Robert Penn Warren). Shakespeare's histories, of course, are a good place to start a discussion about fictionalized accounts of real events.

We can all agree that lying for personal gain or lying to hurt others is wrong, and we can also agree that journalists have a responsibility to pursue truth by reporting facts. The purpose of striving for objectivity in journalism is to keep emotion or politics from obscuring or perverting fact. But what if the culprit is objectivity? It might not be too far of a stretch to incorporate a discussion of New Journalism and Creative Nonfiction into your teaching.

New Journalism emerged in the late 1960s and early 1970s. It's interesting to discuss with the students what was attractive about this kind of "true" storytelling. Hunter S. Thompson famously said, "You can't be objective about Nixon." The practitioners of New Journalism engage in the telling of real events using the conventions of fiction. Some of those conventions include descriptions of personal experience and a lack of objectivity. Oftentimes, the author will show up in the work, and dialogue will be related as if overheard word for word when the author could not be giving a firsthand account. Works of New Journalism you might consider assigning include Tom Wolfe's *The Electric Kool-Aid Acid Test*, Hunter S. Thompson's *Fear and Loathing in Las Vegas*, Truman Capote's *In Cold Blood*, and Norman Mailer's *The Armies of the Night*. Shorter pieces by these authors also might work for your purposes.

In addition to New Journalism, there are now departments in creative writing programs—places where writers go to study the writing of poetry, short stories, novels, plays, screenplays, etc.—with the title of "Creative Nonfiction" (alternatively, "Literary Journalism" or "Narrative Journalism"). Their discussions revolve around the question of how to relate nonfiction stories creatively. Most of what writers of creative nonfiction produce falls under the heading of memoir. Writers such as David Sedaris, Sebastian Junger, John Krakauer, Joan Didion, Augusten Burroughs, Anne Lamott, and Joyce Maynard, although in much different ways on much different subjects, tell stories in which they try to recapture real events.

This is not the end to the list of ways to connect Tim O'Brien to your curriculum. As we've shown in the preceding pages, *The Things They Carried* and stories from it, in addition to *If I Die in a Combat Zone*, *Going After Cacciato*, *The Nuclear Age*, and *In the Lake of the Woods*, have fit well for us into studies of literature and writing as core and companion texts, discussion starters, and lesson plan lead-ins. Our intention with this chapter—as with this book as a whole—is to show teachers what we've come up with toward the goal of providing you with jumping-off points for engaging your students in the study and discussion of Tim O'Brien's multifaceted works.

A Chronology of Tim O'Brien's Works

1973   *If I Die in a Combat Zone, Box Me Up and Ship Me Home*
1975   *Northern Lights*
1978   *Going After Cacciato*
1985   *The Nuclear Age*
1990   *The Things They Carried*
1994   *In the Lake of the Woods*
1998   *Tomcat in Love*
2002   *July, July*

Appendix: Stories and Works by Chapter

The following list does not account for every instance in this book in which a story or work by O'Brien is mentioned. Rather, this list is a guide to those places where we quote from or discuss an idea for teaching a story from *The Things They Carried* or another O'Brien work. You may wish to use this guide as a quick reference when teaching the stories.

Chapter 1: Where Life and Art Intersect
    "The Things They Carried"
    If I Die in a Combat Zone
    "On the Rainy River"

Chapter 2: A True Story That Never Happened
    "How to Tell a True War Story"
    "The Things They Carried"
    "Spin"
    "The Sweetheart of the Song Tra Bong"
    "On the Rainy River"
    "Notes"
    "The Lives of the Dead"
    "Good Form"

Bibliography

BATES, MILTON J. "Men, Women, and Vietnam." *America Rediscovered: Critical Essays on Literature and Film of the Vietnam War.* Ed. Owen W. Gilman, Jr. and Lorrie Smith. New York: Garland, 1990. 27–63.

BEIDLER, PHILIP D. *American Literature and the Experience of Vietnam.* Athens: U of Georgia P, 1982.

BONN, MARIA S. "Can Stories Save Us? Tim O'Brien and the Efficacy of the Text." *Critique* 36 (1994): 2–15.

CALLOWAY, CATHERINE. "'How to Tell a True War Story': Metafiction in *The Things They Carried.*" *Critique* 36 (1995): 249–57.

FUDGE, DENNIS KEITH. *Questioning Truth: War and the Art of Writing in Ambrose Bierce, Stephen Crane, Michael Herr, and Tim O'Brien.* Diss. U of Mississippi, 1996. Ann Arbor: UMI, 1996. 9640312.

GOTTLIEB, ANNIE. "Two Sides of a Modern Disaster." *New York Times on the Web* 1 July 1973. 18 Feb. 2006 <http://www.nytimes.com/books/98/09/20/specials/obrien-combat.html>.

HANNA, JULIA. "The Things He Carries." *Kennedy School Bulletin* Spring 2003. 1 May 2006 <http://www.ksg.harvard.edu/ksgpress/bulletin/spring2003/features/things.html>.

HARRIS, ROBERT R. "Too Embarrassed Not to Kill." Rev. of *The Things They Carried,* by Tim O'Brien. *New York Times* 11 Mar. 1990. 25 June 2007 <http://query.nytimes.com/gst/fullpage.html?res=9C0CE5D F1039F932A25750C0A966958260&sec=&spon=&pagewanted =print>.

HEBERLE, MARK A. *A Trauma Artist: Tim O'Brien and the Fiction of Vietnam.* Iowa City: U of Iowa P, 2001.

HELLMANN, JOHN. *American Myth and the Legacy of Vietnam.* New York: Columbia UP, 1986.

HEPOLA, SARAH. "Telling War Stories: Tim O'Brien, Tequila, and a Few Late Nights." *Austin Chronicle* 1 May 2000. 28 Apr. 2006 <http://weeklywire.com/ww/05-01-00/austin_books_feature.html>.

HERZOG, TOBEY C. *Tim O'Brien.* Twayne's United States Authors Ser. New York: Twayne, 1997.

————. *Vietnam War Stories: Innocence Lost.* London: Routledge, 1992.

JAGO, CAROL. *Sandra Cisneros in the Classroom: "Do Not Forget to Reach."* Urbana, IL: National Council of Teachers of English, 2002.

KAPLAN, STEVEN. *Understanding Tim O'Brien.* Columbia: U of South Carolina P, 1995.

LEE, DON. "About Tim O'Brien: A Profile." *Ploughshares* Winter 1995–96: 196–201.

LINDBLOOM, JAMES. "The Heart Under Stress: Interview with Author Tim O'Brien." *Gadfly Magazine* Mar. 1999. 3 May 2006 <http://www.chss.montclair.edu/english/furr/Vietnam/timobgadfly interview0399.html>.

LOOSE, JULIAN. "The Story That Never Ends." *Times Literary Supplement* (No. 4552) 29 June–5 July 1990: 705.

MELLING, PHILIP H. *Vietnam in American Literature.* Boston: Twayne, 1990.

NEILSON, JIM. *Warring Fictions: American Literary Culture and the Vietnam War Narrative.* Jackson: UP of Mississippi, 1998.

O'BRIEN, TIM. "A Conversation with Tim O'Brien." Interview with Daniel Bourne and Debra Shostak. *Artful Dodge* 2 Oct. 1991. 15 Mar. 2006 <http://www.wooster.edu/artfuldodge/interviews/obrien.htm>.

————. *Going After Cacciato.* New York: Delacorte/S. Lawrence, 1978.

————. *If I Die in a Combat Zone, Box Me Up and Ship Me Home.* 1973. New York: Broadway Books, 1999.

————. *In the Lake of the Woods.* 1994. New York: Penguin, 1995.

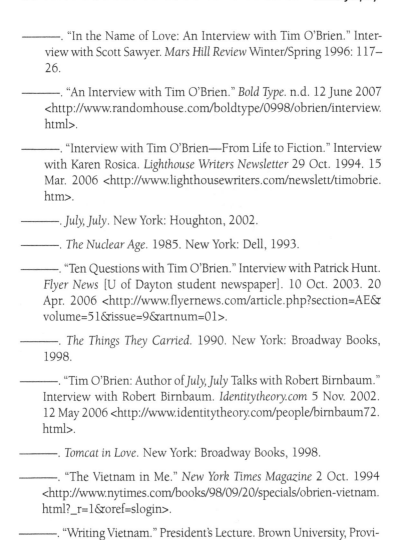

————. "In the Name of Love: An Interview with Tim O'Brien." Interview with Scott Sawyer. *Mars Hill Review* Winter/Spring 1996: 117–26.

————. "An Interview with Tim O'Brien." *Bold Type*. n.d. 12 June 2007 <http://www.randomhouse.com/boldtype/0998/obrien/interview.html>.

————. "Interview with Tim O'Brien—From Life to Fiction." Interview with Karen Rosica. *Lighthouse Writers Newsletter* 29 Oct. 1994. 15 Mar. 2006 <http://www.lighthousewriters.com/newslett/timobrie.htm>.

————. *July, July*. New York: Houghton, 2002.

————. *The Nuclear Age*. 1985. New York: Dell, 1993.

————. "Ten Questions with Tim O'Brien." Interview with Patrick Hunt. *Flyer News* [U of Dayton student newspaper]. 10 Oct. 2003. 20 Apr. 2006 <http://www.flyernews.com/article.php?section=AE&volume=51&issue=9&artnum=01>.

————. *The Things They Carried*. 1990. New York: Broadway Books, 1998.

————. "Tim O'Brien: Author of *July, July* Talks with Robert Birnbaum." Interview with Robert Birnbaum. *Identitytheory.com* 5 Nov. 2002. 12 May 2006 <http://www.identitytheory.com/people/birnbaum72.html>.

————. *Tomcat in Love*. New York: Broadway Books, 1998.

————. "The Vietnam in Me." *New York Times Magazine* 2 Oct. 1994 <http://www.nytimes.com/books/98/09/20/specials/obrien-vietnam.html?_r=1&oref=slogin>.

————. "Writing Vietnam." President's Lecture. Brown University, Providence. 21 Apr. 1999.

PALAIMA, THOMAS G. "Courage and Prowess Afoot in Homer and the Vietnam of Tim O'Brien." *Classical and Modern Literature* 20.3 (2000): 1–22.

PALEY, GRACE. "Digging a Shelter and a Grave." *New York Times on the Web* 17 Nov. 1985. 3 Oct. 2005 <http://www.nytimes.com/books/98/09/20/specials/obrien-nuclear.html>.

RADELICH, MICHAEL A. *Imagining the Truth: Narrative Structure and Technique in the Works of Tim O'Brien.* Diss. U of Nebraska-Lincoln, 1998. Ann Arbor: UMI, 2004. 9903782.

RINGNALDA, DON. *Fighting and Writing the Vietnam War.* Jackson: UP of Mississippi, 1994.

SHEPPARD, R. Z. "Need for Faces." *Time* 19 March 1990 <http://www.time.com/time/magazine/article/0,9171,969628,00.html>.

SMITH, LORRIE N. "'The Things Men Do': The Gendered Subtext in Tim O'Brien's *Esquire* Stories." *Critique* 36 (1994): 16–40.

TEGMARK, MATS. *In the Shoes of a Soldier: Communication in Tim O'Brien's Vietnam Narratives.* Uppsala, Sweden: Uppsala U, 1998.

TIM O'BRIEN, NOVELIST. Tim O'Brien's Home Page. 24 February 2006. 4 May 2006 <http://www.illyria.com/tobhp.html>.

VERNON, ALEX. "Salvation, Storytelling, and Pilgrimage in Tim O'Brien's *The Things They Carried.*" *Mosaic* 36 (2003): 171–88.

———. *Soldiers Once and Still: Ernest Hemingway, James Salter, and Tim O'Brien.* Iowa City: U of Iowa P, 2004.

Authors

Barry Gilmore teaches AP English Literature, International Studies, Facing History and Ourselves, and AP Comparative Government at Lausanne Collegiate School in Memphis, Tennessee, and has also taught at the Tennessee Governor's School for International Studies during the summer for the past ten years. He is the author of three books for teachers: *"Is It Done Yet?" Teaching Adolescents the Art of Revision* (2007), *Speaking Volumes: How to Get Students Discussing Books—and Much More* (2006), and *Drawing the Line: Creative Writing through the Visual and Performing Arts* (1999), as well as numerous articles in publications such as *Tennessee English Journal*, *Teaching Tolerance*, and anthologies from Teachers & Writers Collaborative. He has received teaching awards from Lausanne Collegiate School, the Shelby Memphis Council of Teachers of English, the National Council of Teachers of English, Prentice Hall, and the U.S. Department of Education, including the Presidential Scholars Teacher Recognition Award and the American Star Teacher Award. Gilmore also serves as president of the Tennessee Council of Teachers of English.

Alexander Kaplan was born and raised in Memphis, Tennessee. Graduating from Dartmouth College with an AB in government in 1993, he worked over the next several years as a campus organizer, an environmental campaign director, a bookseller, an editor, a freelance writer, a grant writer, a teacher of first-year college writing, a barista, an elementary-level tutor, and an instructor of an SAT-prep course. Somewhere in there, he

Photo by Allison Evans

managed to obtain an MFA in creative writing from Southwest Texas State University. From 2003 to 2006, he taught American literature, AP English Language, creative writing, and short fiction at Lausanne Collegiate School in Memphis. In 2005 he was given the Judith Calvert Warren New Teacher Award by the Shelby Memphis Council of Teachers of English. Kaplan is currently a writer and teacher in Boston.

This book was composed by Electronic Imaging in Berkeley and Interstate.

Typefaces used on the cover include Trebuchet MS and Zurich Ex BT.

The book was printed on 50-lb. Williamsburg Offset paper by Versa Press, Inc.

Printed in the USA
CPSIA information can be obtained
www.ICGtesting.com
W012041140824
4JS00033B/3196